'Christina Moutsou has written an extremely b[...] poignant stories – often quite chilling, and alway[s ...] only the challenges of human development but, [... y to explore] those challenges within the confidential context of the psychoanalytical consulting room. A work of great creativity and enlightenment, composed in a compelling literary style, I recommend these unique stories most warmly.'

– **Professor Brett Kahr**, senior fellow, Tavistock Relationships, Tavistock Institute of Medical Psychology, London, and senior clinical research fellow in Psychotherapy and Mental Health, Centre for Child Mental Health, London

'Christina Moutsou calls upon her considerable experience and expertise as a psychotherapist to combine beautifully the art of relational psychoanalysis with that of story telling in her exciting new book. She demonstrates her sensitivity and sensibility to both in revealing lucid insights into the clinical encounter in an engaging and gripping way. This is a wonderful read not only for counsellors, therapists and psychoanalysts but also for anyone curious about the nature of human relationship. I commend it highly.'

– **Martin Schmidt**, MBPsS, Jungian training analyst, Honorary Secretary and Regional Organiser for Central Europe of The International Association of Analytical Psychology

'We seem to live in a world that no longer preserves confidentiality. It's as if all the secrets are out, everybody bears all. The person of the psychotherapist, however, seems to have stubbornly resisted today's bear-all culture. The person of the psychotherapist may be one of the few personages that still evoke wonder and mystery. They either appear as mind-readers, criminally sane, or crazier than the rest of us. It's hard to see them as just human. But of course we are human and we get into this "impossible profession" because of our own experiences and our own psychological and emotional characters. In a series of short stories, Christina Moutsou parts the veil to internal psychological experience in a new and intriguing way. We learn about the wounds that bring clients to therapy from their own mouths, before hearing how these clients affect their therapists. In *Fictional Clinical Narratives in Relational Psychoanalysis* we don't just go into the patient's world, we go deep into the therapist's experience and learn just how human and wounded they are too. Dr. Moutsou's work is humanising, normalising, and compassionate. A must-read for clinicians and non-clinicians alike, ultimately proclaiming that at the very core, we're all human, because we're all wounded somehow.'

– **Aaron Balick**, PhD, psychotherapist, supervisor and author of *The Little Book of Calm: Tame your anxieties, face your fears, and live free*

'These are thoughtful, intelligent stories based mainly on exchanges in a therapeutic relationship. Christina writes eloquently and insightfully and I was gripped throughout.'

– **Maggie Hamand**, author of *The Resurrection of the Body* and *Creative Writing For Dummies*

Fictional Clinical Narratives in Relational Psychoanalysis

Fictional Clinical Narratives in Relational Psychoanalysis explores the therapeutic space between the patient and therapist in psychoanalysis and the transformative effect of the therapeutic relationship through a collection of twenty-two short stories beginning at a moment of trauma in adolescence. Christina Moutsou illustrates both contemporary clinical issues as well as the relational and intersubjective nature of the therapy relationship.

First, six teenagers narrate in the first person their experience of battling with sexual abuse, eating disorder, body image, the first sexual awakening, loss of a parent and the intricacies of teenage friendship. The stories then unravel years later as adults in the consulting rooms of Ellie and Jake, two middle-aged therapists working in London. The reader is offered an intimate look at how the therapists work through their personal losses and past wounds, while facing their patients' conflicts and dilemmas including adoption, bereavement, pregnancy loss, lack of intimacy in the couple relationship and a diagnosis of borderline personality disorder.

What distinguishes this collection of fictional clinical narratives is the focus on an internal point of view, where the reader is invited to experience first-hand the vicissitudes of the psychoanalytic dialogue and the enduring marks that trauma and loss leave on each member of the therapeutic dyad. The focus here is on how narratives are constructed and deconstructed through the intersubjective dance between the therapist and the patient. Both are transformed in the process. The fictional nature of the stories also allows for the exploration of sensitive issues that are difficult or awkward to explore adequately using direct case studies from real-life examples.

This fascinating and unusual work provides an innovative method of exploring everyday clinical dilemmas, using an accessible, easy to follow narrative path. It is written from a broadly relational perspective but will appeal to all psychoanalysts and psychoanalytic psychotherapists, as well as to the wider public.

Christina Moutsou is a social anthropologist and a psychoanalytic psychotherapist working in private practice in London, UK. She is co-editor of *The Mother in Psychoanalysis and Beyond* (with Rosalind Mayo, Routledge, 2016) and the author of a psychological novel *Black Cake* published in Greek (Archetypo, 2018). She is a visiting lecturer at Regent's University.

Fictional Clinical Narratives in Relational Psychoanalysis

Stories from Adolescence to the Consulting Room

Christina Moutsou

LONDON AND NEW YORK

First published 2019
by Routledge
2 Park Square, Milton Park, Abingdon, Oxon OX14 4RN

and by Routledge
711 Third Avenue, New York, NY 10017

Routledge is an imprint of the Taylor & Francis Group, an informa business

© 2019 Christina Moutsou

The right of Christina Moutsou to be identified as author of this work has been asserted by her in accordance with sections 77 and 78 of the Copyright, Designs and Patents Act 1988.

All rights reserved. No part of this book may be reprinted or reproduced or utilised in any form or by any electronic, mechanical, or other means, now known or hereafter invented, including photocopying and recording, or in any information storage or retrieval system, without permission in writing from the publishers.

Trademark notice: Product or corporate names may be trademarks or registered trademarks, and are used only for identification and explanation without intent to infringe.

British Library Cataloguing in Publication Data
A catalogue record for this book is available from the British Library

Library of Congress Cataloging in Publication Data
Names: Moutsou, Christina, author.
Title: Fictional clinical narratives in relational psychoanalysis : stories from adolescence to the consulting room / Christina Moutsou.
Description: Abingdon, Oxon ; New York, NY : Routledge, 2019. | Includes bibliographical references and index.
Identifiers: LCCN 2018019606 (print) | LCCN 2018022143 (ebook) | ISBN 9780429456299 (Master) | ISBN 9780429851308 (Web PDF) | ISBN 9780429851292 (ePub) | ISBN 9780429851285 (Mobipocket/Kindle) | ISBN 9781138315471 (hardback : alk. paper) | ISBN 9781138315495 (pbk. : alk. paper) | ISBN 9780429456299 (ebk)
Subjects: | MESH: Professional-Patient Relations | Psychoanalytic Therapy | Psychological Trauma—therapy | Fictional Works
Classification: LCC RC506 (ebook) | LCC RC506 (print) | NLM WM 62 | DDC 616.89/17—dc23
LC record available at https://lccn.loc.gov/2018019606

ISBN: 978-1-138-31547-1 (hbk)
ISBN: 978-1-138-31549-5 (pbk)
ISBN: 978-0-429-45629-9 (ebk)

Typeset in Times New Roman
by Swales & Willis Ltd, Exeter, Devon, UK

To George with love and gratitude for a life together and for Marcus and Violet, the most precious gifts ever

Disclaimer

All characters and situations encountered in this collection of short stories are entirely fictional. Therefore, any resemblance to real people and situations is coincidental.

Contents

Acknowledgements	xi
Introduction	1

PART I
A moment in my teenage years — 9

On the beach	11
The divorce	15
Disclosure	19
The ham and cheese sandwich	26
Awakening	31
London in August, or Serendipity	39

PART II
Ellie — 45

Mess	47
At arm's length	52
The secret	59
$1 + 1 = 0$	66
Lost love and how to find it	74
Flat landscape	79
Clinical polygamy	89

PART III
Jake   95

The crumpled coat   97
Life's meaning   103
Three in bed   108
Driven   114
No words   119
Another chance   124
The scar   136
Love actually   142

PART IV
Ellie and Jake   151

On losing and not being lost   153

Acknowledgements

As with any piece of creative work, there were a number of people who helped me and inspired me along the way. I would like to thank Maggie Hamand and the students and other teachers in her creative writing seminars for invaluable input and much inspiration. Maggie in particular was meticulous in her reading of the manuscript, and her comments really made a difference. I would also like to thank Madeleine Dimitroff and Sally Curtis in my writers' group for providing a hospitable and benign environment to discuss the stories. Sarah King and Sofia Makri read many of the stories, and their input from the point of view of the general reader was invaluable. Jane Haynes and Martin Schmidt read two of the adolescent stories and they were both encouraging and supportive, as well as able to give me feedback from a clinical point of view. I am particularly grateful to Rosalind Mayo and Chrysa Tsoukis for reading many of the stories and taking the time to go through the whole manuscript and give me feedback at short notice. It would be a lonely professional existence without colleagues and friends like them. George Kapetanios has been as always a dedicated reader and very generous in making space for me and my writing during family holidays. I am profoundly grateful to all my patients for making me a therapist and for allowing me to be their companion on the therapy journey. Finally, I would like to thank Kate Hawes and Charles Bath at Routledge for all their support with the project. I am very grateful to Kate Hawes in particular for giving me the chance to experiment and expand into a relatively new and unexplored area, that of fictional therapy writing.

Introduction

While writing about the therapy relationship, Carl Jung stated:

> The meeting of two personalities is like the contact of two chemical substances: if there is any reaction, both are transformed.
>
> (Jung, 1944 (1933): 49–50)

Jung's observation in 1933 sounds surprisingly contemporary, yet it was written well before the relational movement in psychoanalysis was even conceived, and at a time when psychoanalysis was attempting to establish itself as a science. Jung's statement is also a reminder of the importance of 'chemistry', in the sense of reaction and movement in all our close one-to-one encounters. At the core of the present collection of twenty-two stories is the desire to relate, to attach and to become known to one another. Though all encounters in these stories whether within or outside the consulting room are fictional, fiction writing here serves as the vehicle for capturing the ordinary setting of the interpersonal dance of relationships.

The writing of stories in the consulting room is not a new medium for exploring psychoanalytic work and demystifying what goes on between the therapist and the patient, as well as the transformative and creative journey entailed in the analytic process. Irvin Yalom's clinical tales, as he calls them, highlight important aspects of human existence and the form they take within the therapy encounter, especially in relation to mortality, freedom and choice (Yalom, 1999). As in Yalom's stories, Christopher Bollas, has also depicted similar dilemmas and struggles around the therapist's confrontation with mortality and entanglements in his humorous novella, *Dark at the End of the Tunnel*, through his main character, the psychoanalyst (Bollas, 2004). Kennedy's couch tales, on the other hand, are an interesting description of human complexity and suffering, sometimes adopting an omniscient point of view, which is, perhaps, not congruent with a more relational approach, and more reminiscent of traditional case-study writing (Kennedy, 2009).

More recently, in the UK, Stephen Grosz (2013) in his book, *The Examined Life*, has been very successful in demonstrating both the ordinariness and the profound nature of the therapeutic relationship in a series of short stories from his consulting room. The book became a bestseller, in my view, for this very reason.

In 2016, Susie Orbach participated in a series on Radio 4, where actors improvised on fictional case studies, while she saw them for a brief session in her consulting room. The series has been transcribed into a short volume entitled *In Therapy* (2016). Again, Orbach's stories depict ordinary, and yet complex dilemmas which people take to therapy, and the multiple challenges they present to the therapeutic encounter. At the core of her approach is a relational understanding of therapy, which was easy to observe in the Radio 4 series, i.e., how she struggled to respond thoughtfully and honestly to each patient, at the same time making the space for their presenting issues to unfold.

I would say that the present stories are closer in their style and understanding of the therapy encounter to Susie Orbach's relational and fictional approach. Yet, an attempt is made to enliven the main characters of each story, both therapist and patient, through paying close attention to the therapist's subjective experience, and also, to how the environment in which the protagonists meet acts as a container and a symbol of each particular encounter.

There are five important strands at the core of the present collection of fictional short stories in adolescence and in the consulting room: (1) the emphasis on the relational, i.e., recognising the attempt to establish and desire for close relationship as the centre of the therapy encounter; (2) countertransference, in the sense of focusing on the therapist's subjective experience of each therapy encounter; (3) the importance of narrative and meaning, as it is on the unfolding of the patient's story that the therapeutic relationship is built; (4) complexity and chaos, as opposed to causality and an attempt at an objective or 'scientific' understanding of the therapy encounter; and finally, (5) the primacy of literature, in the sense of using description of characters, the environment and inner dialogue in order to depict the highly nuanced complexity of the therapy encounter. Below, I will explore briefly each of these strands.

The relational

There is extensive recent literature on the so-called relational movement in psychotherapy, but not always a consensus on what 'the relational' means in the context of psychoanalysis. My understanding of relational psychotherapy is closer to the understanding of the relational as highlighted by Loewenthal (2014). This is a broader understanding, which stresses the importance of the therapeutic encounter as an intersubjective relationship and a 'being with' the patient. It also places the emphasis on the transformation which takes place for the therapist through the encounter with each patient in the consulting room. According to Loewenthal such understanding of the relational entails the centrality of the therapy relationship; therapy as a 'two-way street'; the vulnerability of both therapist and patient; the importance of countertransference informing the therapeutic dialogue; and lastly, the co-construction and multiplicity of meaning (2014: 4). Loewenthal also emphasises three distinct aspects of such relationality which are: intersubjectivity; the relationship between the subjects (in this case therapist and patient) and the environment; and the relationship between subject (in this case the therapist) and method (basically keeping some critical distance from the application of theory). I think all the above are central elements of the fictional short stories in this collection. Fiction, unlike case-study writing, can focus on the therapist's unprocessed subjective experience and free-flowing thought process in the here and now, it can pay direct attention to the environment, to the potential for defensive use of method as well as to the co-construction of meaning as part of the therapeutic dialogue.

Countertransference

Another theme central in the stories as well as in psychoanalysis is the understanding of countertransference. Again, countertransference has a long history, beginning with Freud's view of it as a hindrance to the psychoanalytic process and a sign that the therapist needed further analysis (1957 (1910)). In the relational paradigm, countertransference is placed within the intersubjective field of the psychic reality of both parties of the therapeutic dyad. In a recent publication on the history of countertransference, Stefana (2017) describes the trajectory from Freud's understanding of countertransference as hindrance, to the emphasis on projective identification in Kleinian theory and the early object relations school, to a second phase in the objects relations school more informed by Winnicott's work and viewing countertransference as the therapist's subjectivity in relation to the patient. More specifically, he mentions the work of Christopher Bollas and how, according to him, the therapist gets a glimpse of the patient's 'real self' through his or her subjective response to the patient while being with them (Stefana, 2017: 116–117). This is precisely the aspect of therapeutic work highlighted in the stories through focusing the narrative on a close first-person point of view of the therapist. In many of the short stories in this collection, the therapist enters a kind of reverie, which invariably tunes into profound experiences in the patient's past and unfolding narrative.

Narrative and meaning

Narrative, in the form of story-telling, and the co-construction of meaning are central parts of therapy work. Lichtenberg (2017) points out the multifaceted nature of narrative, as story-telling always takes place within a particular context, i.e., a story is told at a particular time in the therapy, it is often repeated and in constant change, as aspects of it may be left out or added later on. It may also include a master narrative confirming one's identity such as, for example, the discovery of one's sexual identity at a key point in adolescence (2017: 27). Lichtenberg points out that much of the narrative that takes place as part of the therapeutic dialogue is also non-verbal and uses the environment and the bodily senses in order to construct meaning often taking the form of private lived experience and reverie. He argues that the co-construction of meaning in the therapy relationship is parallel but entwined, i.e., the patient may draw different meaning from the therapist in the narrating of a particular story. What he is referring to here is technique and interpretation, as the therapist will look out for themes and repetitive patterns in the patient's narrative, while the patient may derive different meaning from a particular story such as what his/her feelings are in relation to the narrative according to the therapist's verbal and non-verbal responses (2017: 35–38). Though I agree that the construction of meaning in therapy may be parallel within the therapeutic dyad, and also, incongruent, I also think that there is almost always a dance that takes place between the patient and the therapist and which has to be, partly at least, based on attunement. In the present collection of stories, incongruence and attunement are demonstrated through the subjective experience of the therapist in relation to a particular patient. Also, concurrently with Lichtenberg's statement, narrative in the stories is often non-verbal, situated in the body and in the senses as well as intertwining the past and the present and highlighting aspects of one's history and development.

Complexity and chaos

In a remarkably original book, Galatzer-Levy (2017) uses concepts from nonlinear dynamics and chaos and complexity theory in mathematics to argue against theory building based on linearity and causality in psychoanalysis. He remarks that psychoanalytic theory making has the tendency to rely on knowledge and causality as a way of explaining the patient's symptoms and expecting development to take a linear form. The same applies in the tendency within psychoanalysis to interpret the history and development of the patient in a causal way following a predictable path. Through looking at chaos theory and nonlinear models in mathematics, Galatzer-Levy provides many fascinating examples of unpredictable factors that can affect development in both the childhood of the patient (and the therapist) and the here and now of the therapeutic relationship. I see fiction writing and literature, concurrently with the way I have built the stories in this collection, as prime examples of dynamic nonlinearity and complexity and chaos. For example, the flower arrangement in the consulting room which is no longer provided by the therapist's partner is both symbolic of loss and the death of a once close relationship, a situation which resonates with both therapist and patient, but is also a factor of chaos, i.e., it neither causes nor results in a certain outcome in the therapeutic relationship, yet it can unpredictably affect and speed its development.

The primacy of literature

Concurrently with a turning away from causality, the writing of Adam Phillips is well known for drawing upon literary characters, such as Shakespeare's Othello, to highlight fundamental experiences in human existence which are also at the core of psychoanalytic work. In his latest book, *In Writing*, Phillips stresses the primacy of literature in relation to psychoanalysis precisely because of the ability of literature to capture in words the poetics of human encounters. However, he, indirectly, highlights that such poetics are also present and at the centre of the psychoanalytic encounter. For example, he poignantly describes the encounter between Freud and the poet and novelist H. D. as one where they each enjoyed the other's presence, despite the incongruence in their respective views, Freud seeking theory building through causality and H. D. being concerned with stories and the use of words (Phillips, 2017: 25–31). Perhaps, such incongruence was not as significant as one may be led to believe in that it was the encounter and what each of the two parties made of it through words and the felt senses, which words can only partly capture, that resonated for both.

This also brings me to the importance of literary characters and their points of view in the understanding of the central themes and the forms human distress can take within particular historical and socio-cultural contexts. Through the analysis of four contemporary novels which have as a central character a female villain, Valdré identifies a recent cultural shift which now represents women as central characters in the acquisition of power and the denial of the intimacy and vulnerability that close relationships entail (Valdré, 2017).

Of course, therapists are presented with various forms of stories in the consulting room, yet, unlike in literature, they are often inhibited from seeing their patients as central characters in a novel which depicts unresolved aspects of life. The stories in this collection are unashamedly contemporary. They attempt to capture aspects of human experience within the locality of two therapists, who are both relatively young professionally, though middle-aged in private life. Both therapists' practices are situated in central London.

Twenty-two short stories in adolescence and in the consulting room

The present collection of short stories is written in its entirety in the first person. As argued above, writing in the first person aims to highlight subjective experience, as opposed to objective understanding. The reader is invited to live in the mind of the main character of each story and see the world through their eyes.

This collection of short stories is composed of four parts. Each story in all four parts of the book is preceded by a short introduction which asks open questions linked with the main themes of the particular story. The description at the beginning of each story aims to guide the reader to areas of clinical and theoretical interest, but also to hopefully generate inference and expansion of the questions asked through the reading of the story.

The first six stories in Part I of the collection offer a close-up view of six different teenagers' experiences during a key moment in their adolescence. Such moments tend to divide the teenager's life into the time before and the time after, as they could either be called traumatic, such as the sudden loss of a parent, or they profoundly transform the young person's understanding of self. Six teenagers describe the world through their eyes. The first five teenagers will be met later on, in Parts II and III, as adults in the consulting room. The last story in Part I is written from the point of view of an adult, having frequent flashbacks revisiting her last year in high school through her chance encounter with an old friend she had last seen when she was seventeen. Some of the issues explored in Part I are the death of a parent, divorce, sexual abuse, sexual awakening, intergenerational trauma and the strong impact of teenage friendship.

Parts II and III are also written from the therapist's point of view. The therapists, like the patients, in the stories are fictional characters whose felt sense and lived experience the reader is invited to witness and to relate to. As the stories are all written from a close first-person point of view, the experience is meant to be unconstructed, not driven by causality and knowledge, but rooted in the intertwining of the past and the present and in the relational experiences which the therapist is subject to in each particular story.

So, unlike in the previous examples of well-known and well-written clinical short stories, the fictional short stories in this collection aim to evoke an intense experience of subjectivity. Unlike case-study writing, the aim here is not to make sense, interpret and analyse the clinical material with the purpose of building a narrative which aims to demonstrate resolution and therapeutic progress. This is not to say that making sense of the material and some resolution and/or reparation is not part of the narrative in the stories. However, the focus here is on asking important questions about the therapist's lived experience and how it can hopefully mobilise a turbulent process of transformation for both parties in the therapeutic dyad.

Part II comprises seven stories in the consulting room from the point of view of Ellie, a therapist in her early forties who sees patients from a rented consulting room in the City of London. Ellie has issues around trust in close relationships linked with her experience of her mother and her mother's early and unexpected death. Her difficulty in trusting intimacy is in the background of her work with all her patients, but it manifests in a unique way in each therapeutic relationship that she forms. The entanglements, but also the transformative nature of the therapy relationship are the focus of each story. Some of the issues explored in the stories are the erotic transference, the nature of romantic love, family secrets and adoption, deception, illness and dying as well as the therapist's envy in the therapy relationship.

Part III is composed of eight short stories in the consulting room from the point of view of Jake. Jake is also in his early forties. He is in a failing relationship. He and his partner have a toddler son. His consulting room is at home in north-west London and he juggles a busy practice with being a hands-on father. Jake's relationship with his partner disintegrates slowly through the narration of the stories, and this is in the background of his therapy work with different patients. Some of the issues explored in the short stories of Jake's clinical work with patients are psychosomatics, bereavement, self-harm, the crossing of boundaries in the therapy relationship, working with so-called borderline conditions and couples work.

Part IV is composed of one single short story, which brings Ellie and Jake together in a professional development group which they both attend. The group is entitled, 'On losing and not being lost' as loss is at the core of this story as well as of therapy work. The purpose of this last story is to highlight the unconscious connections between people as well as the links between the past and the present, which are an integral part of any profound transformation both in therapy and in human relationships in general. As such, it concludes the collection with a focus on the relational and its vicissitudes.

References

Bollas, C. (2004). *Dark at the End of the Tunnel*. London: Free Association Books.
Freud, S. (1957 (1910)). The future prospects of psycho-analytic therapy. In *The Standard Edition of the Complete Psychological Works of Sigmund Freud*, vol. 11 (ed. James Strachey et al.). London: Hogarth Press.
Galatzer-Levy, R. (2017). *Nonlinear Psychoanalysis: Notes from Forty Years of Chaos and Complexity Theory*. Abingdon: Routledge.
Grosz, S. (2013). *The Examined Life: How We Lose and Find Ourselves*. London: Chatto & Windus.
Jung, C. J. (1944 (1933)). *Modern Man in Search of a Soul*. New York: Routledge.
Kennedy, R. (2009). *Couch Tales: Short Stories*. London: Karnac.
Lichtenberg, J. D. (2017). Narrative and meaning. In *Narrative and Meaning: The Foundation of Mind, Creativity and the Psychoanalytic Dialogue*. (ed. J. D. Lichtenberg, F. M. Lachmann & J. L. Fosshage). London: Routledge.
Loewenthal, D. (2014). The magic of the relational: An introduction to appraising and reappraising relational psychotherapy, psychoanalysis and counselling. In *Relational Psychotherapy, Psychoanalysis and Counselling: Appraisals and Reappraisals* (ed. D. Loewenthal & A. Samuels). London: Routledge.
Orbach, S. (2016). *In Therapy: How Conversations with Psychotherapists Really Work*. London: Profile Books.
Phillips, A. (2017). *In Writing*. London: Hamish Hamilton.
Stefana, A. (2017). *History of Countertransference: From Freud to the British Object Relations School*. Abingdon: Routledge.
Valdré, R. (2017). *Psychoanalytic Perspectives on Women and Power in Contemporary Fiction: Malice, the Victim and the Couple*. Abingdon: Routledge.
Yalom, I. D. (2000). *Momma and the Meaning of Life: Tales of Psychotherapy*. Loughton: Piatkus.

Part I

A moment in my teenage years

> Adolescence is a pivotal time for forming one's identity and for psychic development. Though this fact is recognised clinically (many therapy resources are dedicated to offering counselling to teenagers and young adults), psychoanalysis focuses on the early years as pivotal for the formation of the ego. Yet, it is in adolescence that the dark forces, perhaps first encountered at the beginning of life, often get unleashed. This collection of six adolescent stories is written in the first person, attempting to offer close-up insight into the experience of turbulence and psychic fragility during adolescence. All stories focus on a moment of trauma which divides life into the time before and the time after.

On the beach

> What is the boundary between teenage play and experimentation and abuse? As a society, we have a complex relationship with abuse, especially in its sexual form. We often fail to name it for what it is, and in doing so, we perpetuate the cycle of shaming the victim, covering abuse over with secrecy and indirectly perpetuating the vicious circle of both the victim and perpetrator remaining unprotected. Research indicates that sexual abuse often takes place between children as well as within the family. The story below is a close-up glimpse of the intrusive and violating nature of sexual abuse as well as how difficult it is to stop it.

Late afternoon of the last day in August on my favourite beach in Chalkidiki. A long golden strip of fine sand ending in the green wooden cabins by the pointy rocks I loved to climb on. The sun had mellowed, its rays hitting the water and the hot sand sideways. I went for a swim. Water was my element, my realm, where I felt alive. Diving under, swirling around, expertly moving up and down. Head down, legs up, lying on my back at the bottom of the sea staring at the sun rays spreading colours on the surface of the water, turning it golden. I floated up to the surface, took a long breath in, water dripping down my face, sticking to my eyelashes, forming rainbows in front of my eyes.

I nearly gasped as I made out Petros's silhouette on my journey up to the foamy water surface. He had followed me in. He was there, waiting for me to come up. Only the bottom of the sea was safe, only there my body belonged to me, only there me and my body were at one. He got hold of my shoulders.

'I can dip you in', he laughed.

'No, you can't', I cried.

I swam, kicking my legs back, raising foam high, hoping it would get into his eyes. He got hold of my legs now, and with his arms around my waist, he tried to swirl me around.

'Come on, let's dive in together', he said.

I held my nose, he tried to move my hand away.

'Don't be a baby', he giggled just before going under. 'You don't need to hold your nose, just breathe the water out.'

'I like diving alone', I mumbled, but there we were, going down together, his arms firm around me, dragging me down, our bodies intertwined.

I breathed water in through my nose. It made me dizzy. Out of my depth. I knew what this felt like from before. He was hiding behind the white lacy curtains in our living room, the big fluffy plum-coloured sofa turning darker under the dimming light of dusk. Where was everybody? Where was Mother? What was I doing alone in the dark living room? Were we playing hide and seek? He jumped in front of me from behind the curtains. I let out a little scream that seemed to amuse him. 'Touch', he said. He was holding a batch of matches, their tips black, burned. I did. They were hot. I stepped back and cried. He laughed with delight. 'Cry baby!' he hummed. Did I run to Mother?

Panic set in; what had been my element a minute ago was going to drown me to death. Underwater, I could feel his tongue trying to push into my mouth and something firm pressing against my belly. I kicked my legs hard to come to the surface, gasping for air.

Mother was lying on her back sunbathing, her eyes firmly shut. For all the time I had been chased after in the sea, she had not moved or opened her eyes once – or had she?

'I am getting out now', I said. I was feeling defeated. Here I was, being banished from my realm of the sea, being chased out of it onto the hot sand, to feel the boredom of aloneness. Then I noticed her, the old lady discreetly observing us, her eyes following us as we moved about treading turquoise water.

'Come on, one more dip', he said. 'Have a jump from my shoulders.'

Father had a soft spot for him, I remembered. 'The first, the only boy in the family', Father always said. I felt like saying, 'but he is not part of our family', but I never did. Father always knew best. He and Petros spent time together doing boys' things. They would go out holding a ball, they would come back hours later carrying shiny red cars and ride-on toys and, once, a cowboy dress-up costume. I knew then that being a girl could not ever be as exciting. I was Father's favourite, or so he said, but we never came back home together, our faces glittering with conspiracy and fun. Father sometimes had private talks with him. Talks in whispering voices full of intensity. It was adult stuff that he was teaching him, Father would tell me, if I tried to join in, and I would know better than to stay in the room with them for more than five minutes.

He looked very much like Father, or so other people said. I could never see what they saw. Father was dressed in smooth suits, their fine material enveloping elegantly his body. Father smelled of discreet cologne and freshly applied aftershave. His voice was deep and commanding. His voice was tender and warm and bubbly. Father was not clumsy, spotty and full of sweat. The problem was that Petros thought he was like Father too and, like him, he could give me orders, tell me what to do, and I would. The problem was that I could not say no.

He dived behind me, his head coming up between my legs, his arms gripping my thighs firmly. I was being raised high, riding on his shoulders.

'Ready, steady . . . go!'

Here I was, falling backwards in the water, feeling whole again. I stayed at the bottom for as long as I could hold my breath, as deep as I could, no body part coming through to the surface. He was there when I came up, waiting to grab me.

'Hello, my chubby dolphin', he cackled, grabbing hold of my shoulders.

I turned my head to look for the lady. She was still there, staring at us.

'Come on, a last dip', he said, pressing me against his body.

I felt the old lady's gaze burning my back.

'This time we go down as one body, stuck together, OK?' he said, his breath becoming short.

He got his legs around my hips and trapped me tight against his body. Before our heads were under, I could feel his lips pressing against mine, his tongue full of saliva going deep into my mouth, his bad breath. As soon as we were under, water started filling my mouth. I swallowed hard and almost choked. I kicked against his groin, finally came up, gasping for air.

The lady was there by our side, her expression stern, austere.

'Children,' she said, 'how old are you?'

I could tell from her tone and use of language that she was a well-educated, probably cultured woman.

'Let's swim away', he whispered in my ear while I was still trying to catch my breath.

'Children,' she repeated firmly, 'are you here unsupervised?'

'No,' I mumbled, 'my mother is over there.'

I pointed at the woman in the black swimming suit, lying still on her back, her eyes firmly shut.

'I am going to have to go and talk to her,' she said, 'because the things you are doing are just not right for children to do. I suggest you follow me out of the sea now, if you don't want to be in even more trouble.'

He shrugged his shoulders and swam off. I swam slowly towards the shore, letting the lady get out of the sea first. I hesitantly got out of the water, but rather than follow the lady to the umbrella where Mother was lying unperturbed, I sat on the hot sand, two metres away, turning my back to them, looking at the pale horizon merging with the deep dark blue far away. My ears tried to get hold of the broken syllables through the breezy wind, the shrieks of nearby children and the soft lapping of the water on the sand near my feet.

'Sorry to disturb you, madam,' the lady said, 'but I have been watching your children for some time now, and I am very concerned about what they are doing. Are they both your children?'

'He is my nephew, from my husband's side . . .', I could hear Mother mumble.

'So, they are first cousins. And how old are they?'

'My daughter is eleven, he is nearly sixteen. What's this about?'

'Well, they are far too young to be kissing on the mouth and they are first cousins too. I have to say I am very concerned. . . . Have you thought about asking your daughter to tell you what's going on?'

'Oh, I would not worry as much, madam . . . can be naughty . . . they are only children . . . please . . . own business . . .'

I stood up and walked towards the umbrella as soon as the lady had turned her back, a sense of foreboding heavy in my stomach.

'It's time to go home', Mother told me coldly.

I took a deep breath in, a salty bitter taste overwhelming my mouth. The taste of the sea had now turned into the taste of his dirty saliva. I swallowed hard to send away the waves of nausea which gave me goosebumps.

'What was the lady talking to you about?' I dared to ask.

'She said that you were both naughty.' Mother's voice sounded like cold metal. 'You can't help it, Natalie. You have just got your father's blood, a genetic predisposal to all the wrong things in life', she added. Her contempt for me felt like a cake she could not have enough of.

'But . . .'

'You know how much I hate drawing people's attention to us, especially if it is through your filthy actions.'

He came out of the sea just at that minute, when I would either speak up or cry. Words and tears evaporated like burst bubbles under the hot August sun.

'Change into dry clothes now', Mother said to me curtly. 'You look cold.'

I took a look at his hungry gaze. Another shiver ran through me. I felt overcome with nausea.

'I am not taking you out to the beach with us again, Petro', she told him sternly. 'You have been naughty.'

I collected my clothes and a towel. 'I'm going to the changing rooms', I whispered to her.

I walked where the water reached the sand turning it into smooth, silky mud. I let my feet dip into it and felt the little pebbles that embroidered it tickle my soles. 'Just like Father.' I was getting confused. Was it Petros or I or both of us that were like him? And if it were both of us, did that mean that we were both the same? 'Filthy.' The nausea came back. I felt like dipping into the sea again, swimming to the deep this time, so nobody would know where I was. The soft pile of clothes hanging round my bent arm stopped me. The sun had started to turn orange; its sideways rays fell burning on my skin. I needed to get out of here.

The changing rooms were at the other end of the beach; five green wooden cabins smelling of seawater, sand and urine. I loved the scent of wood and sea mixing together, but I would always try to block out the acidic smell of urine rising from the ground. When I was a breath away from the first empty cabin, a hand tapped on my shoulder.

'I'm here', he said, huffing and puffing. 'Nobody can see us here.'

I ran for the cabin and quickly slammed the door shut behind me. I forced the metal hook on the round rusty ring attached to the door, just before he had time to push in.

The divorce

> It is both easy and customary to pathologise teenagers and to attribute labels to their distress such as suffering from anorexia and, later on, possibly a BPD diagnosis. The dynamics in a family that can lead to accumulative distress as well as a sense of emotional isolation for a young person are not always easy to spot. Especially in the context of middle-class and apparently privileged families, teenage angst and self-harming behaviour can look like an internal state of pathology. This story offers insight into a difficult mother–daughter relationship, which feels deeply depriving to the daughter. It offers understanding and empathy with teenage distress rather than focusing on the diagnosis of pathology.

It was the quiet time after our midsummer lunch, when my sister and I were supposed to retreat in our rooms and do some homework, while Mum was getting ready for her evening teaching, English as a foreign language to summer students.

'I will pop into Tracy's for a quick coffee before my lesson', she told me hastily. 'Please, mind your sister.'

She did not seem to notice how I rearranged my food around on my plate, how I slowly chewed the peas one by one, giving the rest of them a gentle push, as though they were a hundred tiny footballs trying to score a goal on the other side of the plate. The chicken was lying almost untouched when I finished, cut up in many small pieces, most of them expertly hidden under the roast potatoes.

'I don't like potatoes any more', I mumbled when we had all finished and she was clearing the plates ready to stack them into the dishwasher.

'That's all right, my darling. Potatoes are not good for our waistline', she said absentmindedly.

I felt a knot in my throat. How could I get to her, if even not eating was a way of joining her club, that of the slim and the fit middle-class and middle-aged mums living in our leafy neighbourhood, who frequented our local Pilates studio and dressed as though they were sixteen at most. She had taken to asking me to join her in our club's swimming pool this summer and I don't know if I imagined it, but it felt like she was keen to show off my slimming figure.

'Such an athletic body you have', she would say. 'A real gift for a growing girl!'

16   The divorce

A couple of her friends had noticed my weight loss.

'Are you on a diet, Bella?' Tracy had asked me when we bumped into her by the swimming pool, looking half interested and half concerned. 'Every time I see you, you look thinner and thinner.'

Mum seemed in a hurry to get rid of her.

'So good to see you, Tracy. We just popped in for a quick swim. Good to see everyone is getting fit this summer', she added in her usual not-stopping-to-take-a-breath way and she squeezed past her to get into the pool.

'She is such a pest', she whispered in my ear as soon as we were in the pool. 'Always wanting us to be best friends, as though we are at nursery school.'

I had not had a period since early spring and in many ways this felt both good and normal. It was a return to a time in my life, my childhood, when Daddy would always have lunch with us and he would wolf his food down, despite Mum's remarks about his unfortunate table manners and his working-class origins. A time when Anna was a little, cute toddler and she used to climb on my lap, plant a wet kiss on my cheek and call me 'her Lelly'. A time when we did not all hide in our rooms and when Dad used to occupy the living room with the TV on, watching his favourite match with a can of lager in his one hand rather than be unseen and unheard of in the house. With the prospect of redundancy lurking over him and his salary reduced, he needed to put in the hours, I had heard him saying to Anna who had climbed on his lap one late evening. She was by far his favourite daughter, the only one who was happy to join him in cheering Man U.

I did not feel like reading today, although reading had been my best place of escape since school had stopped. I could hear Anna tapping her foot, as she was yet again on her PlayStation, but for once, I did not feel the burning guilt in my stomach of trying to save her from Mum's oblivion, trying to be the best possible big sister like my mother always wanted me to. Eight years between us and yet, at times, I knew exactly how she was feeling, the sinking feeling in her heart, as she was trying to lose herself in her digital games, to forget that she had been forgotten.

I spread myself on the sofa and I toyed with the idea of switching the TV on. Surely, Anna would hear and she would be down in a second, asking that we watch a DVD and eat popcorn together snuggled up in front of the TV. Then, any prospect of homework or, at least, of reading her a book, as I had taken to doing every afternoon when Mum was out for her teaching, would be out of the window. Then, we would both sink together in dead-brainland. Besides, I would not want Anna to see me not eating popcorn. She was too young to know any of that. I wanted my little sister to have the life I used to have at eight, a life full of exciting stories that Mum would read to me and trips to cool theatres, museums and parks in central London. Yet, despite my best intentions, I failed to be the good big sister she deserved. Why was I so much better at not eating, let alone the other stuff I would never want her to know about, than at entertaining her?

The other stuff was the only thing that Mum had noticed about me lately, the fresh scars on my arms.

'What is that, Bella?' she said very seriously, pointing to a long straight red line on my upper arm. She had caught me with bare arms, as I was coming out of the bathroom.

'Nothing . . . a scratch . . .'
'It looks nasty and deep to me. How did it happen?'
'I don't know, don't remember', I said trying to move away.
'You wouldn't do something like that to yourself, would you?'
'Give me a break, Mum', I said, finally managing to squeeze past her and lock myself in my room.

She had come to my room a few days later.

'I talked to Tracy', she said. 'Apparently, some adolescent girls, when they are distressed, they do that, cut themselves. Are you distressed about something, Bella?'

I hated it when she referred to Tracy as our in-house psychologist. All she had done was an introductory course to counselling, another favourite middle-class pastime in our area, as I gathered. And how pathetic how she switched to Tracy being her best pal and her confidante when it suited her and how she snubbed her when she was around the cooler crowds living around the park. The truth is I did not know if I was distressed. All I knew was that I was bloody unhappy like everyone else in this family. Everyone else other than her. She seemed to enjoy her life in the leafy London suburbs, a cherished dream hard won over endless arguments with Dad about class and style and the best way to make enough money for the lifestyle we all needed to have.

I decided to go and read Anna a story after all and then gently encourage her to do some homework. It was as I was getting up that I saw it, squashed between two of the plump cushions in our three-seater. How strange, I thought, she forgot her mobile and she has not even come back for it. What if something happened to us? How would we even reach her? I picked it up without knowing why. The message was there on the screen:

You poor thing! I am here for you. Come over for coffee and chat if u have time. Txx

My heart fluttered without knowing why. I slid the arrow at the bottom of her iPhone and to my relief there was no password that I needed to insert. I tapped 'Messages' and it was right there.

Tim says he doesn't love me any more. He is moving out by the end of the week. What am I supposed to tell the girls? I am so gobsmacked! Lxx

I stared at the screen. I was feeling nothing. I felt like pinching myself. Surely, anything would be better than nothing. Eventually, I let her phone drop back on the sofa and, as an afterthought, I pushed it back where it was, squashed between the sofa cushions. She must be on her way back to pick it up, I thought as I was walking like a robot up the stairs.

'Bel, are you coming to play?' I heard Anna shout from her room.

I tried to keep my voice steady. 'No, not today. I've got too much work to do.'

I was almost hoping for some protest, but no sound came from Anna's room other than the electronic whistles from her PlayStation. Why did Mum not register her at a summer club at least?

18 The divorce

'It is a golden opportunity, now that you've got so much studying on, for Anna to catch up on school work as well, she is really behind. You are such a good example for her, my darling Bella', she had told me.

In other words, it was a golden opportunity for me to take Anna on, while she went about doing nothing. I so hated her for all her smoothed-over self-centredness. I waited and waited for the sound of the key at the door, but as my alarm clock showed six pm, it was clear that she was going straight to her lessons. The impulse came as a flush when I popped into the bathroom. The razor was there on my side of the cupboard, where I had left it concealed in the travellers' toothbrush case from last time. I did not have time to think. A quick slice, sharp pain, gush of blood, then feeling whole again, in control, the pain just in my arm, not in the deepest places of me.

'Bel, are you in there? I am so hungry!'

'Mum, will be home soon, she will fix you dinner.'

Panic, the blood is not stopping, what do I do?

'Can you fix me some toast with lots of butter like the other time, Bel? Please?'

'I ll be out in a minute, OK? Can you go now? Please, give me some privacy.'

I hear her disappointed walking away from the bathroom. I am trying very hard to think. How does blood stop? I am sure we did this in a lesson at school. Cold water? That seems to make it a bit better. Squeezing the wound. I am sure this is it. I grab the bathroom towel, roll it and wrap it tight around my arm. Counting to ten, no blood seen through the towel, counting to twenty, I can just about see some pink shade coming through. I dare to remove the towel. The blood seems to be crusting over now. Good! Looking manically in my wardrobe for a convincing outfit. It is bloody hot today. My goth black shirt and cropped jeans will do. Then, I hear the key at the door. She is home at last. I take a deep breath, dare to pop out of my room.

'Mum, are you home?'

'Yes, darling.'

'Can you fix Anna some dinner? She is hungry.'

I stand at the top of the stairs and see her moving aimlessly in our airy and bright open-plan living room.

'Could you fix her something please, Bella?'

'What?'

'I am going out for a drive. Not feeling very well today.'

'Is Dad home soon?'

'Not sure.'

'Please, Mum, Anna needs you.'

'I won't be long, OK. I promise.'

We are hugging tight in Anna's bed, a plate full of crumbs and smeared with butter left on the floor. I can see her eyes glazing as I am reading her a second story. It won't be long before she is finally asleep.

Disclosure

> This story attempts to give insight into how overwhelming and devastating shame is for a teenager's developing identity. Feelings of self-disgust and a negative body image often express deep psychic wounds which do not always concern the individual in question, but which can be transmitted through intergenerational trauma as well as other unprocessed feelings of a parent. Layla, the main character in this story, becomes the container of her mother's self-loathing and mental distress. In doing so, she increasingly loses sense of her own identity while she merges with the projected self-hatred and despair. Another theme in this story is how a complex ethnic identity can play into and reinforce feelings of shame and self-deprecation.

When Mum told me the truth about her childhood during an early autumnal afternoon, my life was divided into the time before and the time after. I still remember the colour of the kitchen couch where I was sitting when Mum told me. It was a worn-out wine-red corduroy. I remember the texture under my fingers, the white spots that I kept trying to brush away, thinking that it was dust or dirt, realising only then that it was actually woven into the shabby material. I don't think that I ever sat on the couch again, it was like the elephant in the room that I made sure remained invisible. After a much needed kitchen revamp just before I was about to leave for college meant that the couch was chucked out and replaced by a freshly painted white bench, I felt like I could breathe more freely in that kitchen again.

That early autumn afternoon when I had just turned twelve, I walked into the kitchen, still in my royal blue and grey school uniform, to ask when tea would be ready, only to find Mum wiping her tears on her apron. My little brothers were playing in the garden, oblivious to the gathering mist and to the emerging autumnal chill. They seemed perfectly happy in their polo school shirts and their rolling-down-the-hips grey school trousers.

It was not the first time that I had found Mum crying alone in the kitchen. In a way, I preferred her sadness to her scorning me. I had always been good at comforting her, and comforting her made me feel like the daughter she had always longed for, the daughter who would be mindful of the house chores and capable of keeping my brothers in good order and out of her sight. Since the beginning of secondary school, I had volunteered to drop them off at school and pick them up on my way back, much to Mum's relief.

Given how good, how perfect I was striving to be and how highly Mum thought of me, at least for most of the time, her scolding always felt like a whack in the face. Even worse, it came at unexpected times when I could not have anticipated that I was doing anything wrong at all. One of the worse times was at the beginning of term, when I had asked Mum if I could invite my newly made friend Alison round for tea after school. I was so proud of myself, so excited! I was not used to making friends easily at all and this time, bang, Alison and I were sitting next to each other in class, full of chat, and Alison had already asked me round to her house, telling me all about her family's endearing cocker spaniel, Fluffy. Little did she know that I was wary of pets, as we never once had any at home.

'How selfish of you!' Mum had snapped. 'Has it ever crossed your mind how busy I get in the afternoons, trying to clean after all of you and prepare supper as well for your father's return at home? What if the house is not tidy enough? I hate people gossiping. Invite her if you must', she had added later in a self-sacrificing tone. 'I will make sure I am out of sight.'

'But, Mummy!' I had protested. 'She will be coming here to meet you!'

'I've had enough of this selfish talk!' Mum said sternly and she walked proudly out of the kitchen and up the stairs into her bedroom.

There were hardly any guests in our house as far back as I could remember. Mum's distaste for Dad's relatives, especially the practising Muslim ones, had quickly established that they were rather spare in our house. Not that this side of his family were eager to visit anyway, as they not only disapproved of his marrying an English wife, but, much worse, choosing to go for a secular wedding instead of demanding that she convert to Islam. In fact, the thought had crossed my mind that Mum was afraid that a new visitor's discerning attention might pick up a hint of 'Muslimness' in the house.

As far as I understood, Mum and Dad's marriage had in fact been willingly secular from both sides. Dad was eager to leave behind his Muslim roots and Mum, the memories of her oppressive Catholic upbringing. The only concession she made was that their first child would acquire an Arabic name. In fact, Mum had claimed that this was one of the few things they had ever agreed on, as she loved the name Layla.

'That way your father can see in you forgotten bits from his culture', she said to me on one of her rare cheerful days, and since then, my name had become yet another boulder on my shoulders. I have often wondered why Mum had married Dad, if the only connection to his origins she could tolerate was in her first child's name. My brothers, on the other hand, had perfectly ordinary English names, Luke and Andrew, and nobody seemed to make a big deal out of what connection they needed to have with Dad's culture.

Looking back, I think that Mum's mood swings deteriorated in the last two years before that fateful day when I was twelve. In fact, the only time we had a guest live in our house, was when I was ten and Mum's dad had come to live with us after Granny passed away suddenly from a stroke. I hardly knew either of them really, and my memories of Grandad staying with us are as grim as the Liverpool sky in late November. Here was a thing I did not get back then or now that I had finally left home for college in faraway and much freer London: why had Mum invited him in, if she disliked him as much as she seemed to?

'It's out of duty, Layla', she would say. 'He's got nobody else in the world and he doesn't know how to take care of himself. He never had to, you see. If I leave him to stay alone, he'll be gone within a month.'

'Can you take him his tea, please, Layla', she would often ask me. 'I can't bear it when he talks to me. He was not such a nice man, he was not that good to me. One day, you will understand.'

His sudden death from cardiac arrest about six months before I turned twelve had come as a relief to all of us. It spared Mum the guilt of having to put him in a nursing home, which I had overheard Mum and Dad arguing about. His death had not done much good to Mum's mood though, neither had it helped things in her struggling relationship with Dad.

'Why should I and my children put up with him, if you can hardly bear him?' I overheard Dad hissing to Mum one late evening in front of the TV. 'We have hardly ever had anyone from my family staying over for more than a night.'

'This is how I was brought up, to be dutiful. I can't change it now. Besides, you have all benefited greatly from my dutifulness', Mum replied, and it was easy to picture the bitter look on her face.

'What about my duty to my culture, then? I am going to register the boys in Saturday Arabic school. I've heard there is quite a liberal one, not far from here. They need to learn about their roots.'

'They won't go, Al', Mum said, stressing her own Anglicised version of Dad's typically Muslim name, 'Ali'. 'Besides, I thought you were not even a Muslim yourself.'

'This is not even about being Muslim. This is about my . . . their cultural origins.'

'Come on you know what Arabic school is about, Al, reciting the Koran. Please do me a favour, don't try to fill their precious developing brains with crap.'

'I see, crap. What about your father's presence, huh? Have you told them how nice he has been to you? Isn't that feeding them crap?'

It was around that time that Dad, normally back at home by six, had started being out until late some evenings. He was frequenting a Moroccan café on the outskirts of Liverpool, Mum said, with much frowning upon.

'He was not exactly ever an intellectual, and surely that will not help his thinking', she had added contemptuously, referring to Dad's lack of university education, another frequent topic of friction between them.

Going to university had been Mum's route of escape from home, but the financial uncertainty that her philosophy degree had given her meant that she had hastily decided to marry at the end of her degree. Dad's secure job as an automobile technician meant that she would never again have to rely on her parents. It was also, of course, a way of getting to them and making sure that there would be a permanent distance between them for the rest of her married life, their relationship consisting of the routine exchange of Christmas and birthday cards and a yearly visit.

'It was also looks', Mum had told me once confidentially in one of our afternoon chats over tea while my brothers played out of sight. 'Looks had lured me into marrying your father. I was seduced by the shine of his emerald green eyes, over dark skin. Such unusual colours he had. You should never let yourself get carried away by somebody's looks, Layla. Beauty is always deceptive.'

In fact, looks, and more precisely, Dad's looks, had been one of my biggest problems for the last two years of primary school. Alison's enthusiastic friendship had somehow made my discomfort and self-consciousness better at the beginning of grammar school, but the truth was that, no matter what, my looks, clumsily passed down by Dad, and definitely in the wrong shape and form, could not be wiped out. I had inherited Dad's dark curly hair, coarse and unruly, as well as his long nose and even worse, much worse, his thick eyebrows and his overall hairiness. Why, just why, could I not have inherited Mum's traditional English looks, her flat and straight dark-blonde hair and her pale, smooth and hairless skin? Neither of my brothers with their English names, straight hair and delicate noses had to endure the questions about religion or the curious looks, let alone the teasing, that I had to, despite sharing the same Arabic surname with me.

In the last year of primary school, I finally dared to say to Mum that perhaps I needed to think about shaving my legs, and I was about to ask her about what were my other options, but Mum had given me one of her scorning looks straight away.

'What do you need to shave your legs for?' she had asked sternly.

'Because I am really standing out from the others.'

'One thing my Catholic upbringing has taught me', she said, 'is that one should be grateful for being given a healthy body.'

'Well, you never had to endure being different, so you wouldn't know what it feels like', I raised my voice. It was one of the very few times I dared to talk to Mum like that, and of course I had lived to regret it. The sulking and stony silence I had to endure in the week that followed made me promise myself never to talk to her like that again.

In fact, it was my audacious reply that Mum brought up again, that early autumn afternoon, when she told me the truth about her origins.

'It was very presumptuous of you to assume, Layla, that I know nothing about standing out. I know a lot about being different, not belonging. In fact, for all my life as a child I was made to feel like a pariah.'

I had heard snippets before about Mum's unhappy childhood, how her parents were too strict and conservative, how lonely and restricted she had felt growing up with them. But not belonging, that did not make much sense to me. Why would Mum, growing up as part of a tightly knit small community, where, according to her, everyone knew everyone, feel that she did not belong? She could not even imagine what it must feel like to go through school without having a single friend knowing your family or coming to play in your house or inviting you over. This is what not belonging *really* felt like.

'If you care to know why I am sometimes sad, I could tell you, now that you are old enough', Mum had continued.

And then, her story unfolded in much more detail than I would have ever wished for. For all the years of my adolescence after that day, and until I reached college in London, a much happier and lighter place to be, as much as I wished for oblivion, all the little details she told me that day that painted Mum's wretched childhood kept creeping in. They were imprinted in my memory like a deep skin tattoo, and even if they explained all too well Mum's frequent sadness and her anger outbursts and why she never wanted to make any friends or trust that anyone liked her, the imprint they left on me was as unsightly as my hairy legs.

'My parents were not my real ones', Mum said. 'I've known since as far back as I can remember. They made a point of telling me how charitable they were to adopt me and rescue me from a life of sin as the daughter of the village whore, a woman who was happy to have sexual relationships out of wedlock. I was the product of such a liaison, they always stressed to me.'

I remember how I wanted to tell her that I felt sorry for her, how much I wanted to comfort her, but I remained speechless, numbness spreading through my limbs.

'Only impeccable manners and a strict Catholic upbringing could wash out the sins of my origins, let alone my faulty nature, my parents would say to me. And my manners, you see, were never impeccable enough, despite the excellent school reports I had always received. For my parents, a girl's place in the world was to be good rather than be clever.'

'How awful!' I managed to mumble.

'And when l fell short of being impeccable, which, according to my parents, would be often enough, my father's beatings that continued well into my teens were perfectly designed to humiliate me and bring it home for good that I was irredeemably, hopelessly bad.'

And here came the worst bit that I wished Mum had spared me, what she called the 'sexual innuendo' of her father's beatings.

'He would ritually take my knickers down, Layla. He would ask me to lie on my stomach, ceremonially taking his trousers' belt down and beating me on my bare bottom until I was red and blue. Men's inherent perversity is in their nature, Layla, they can't help it', she went on, implicating not only her father, who was unquestionably a monster, but mine too in her universal hatred for the male species.

I could see now why, for many years, she slept in a separate bedroom from Dad. She had hinted that her husband had come in many ways to remind her of her own father's sadistic and abusive behaviour. This last disclosure in particular had felt to me like dirt that I was forced to swallow and it had left me with a permanent slimy aftertaste. My memories of Dad from early childhood, though things changed later, as he grew distant, were of a large cuddly teddy bear, and now, after Mum's disclosure, he had started transforming in my mind into a creepy weirdo that I would keep avoiding for the rest of my adolescence.

How time divided in my mind into before and after Mum's disclosure was much to do with shame. Before Mum's disclosure, I was somewhat awkward, but still contended to be, by all accords, a nice, cute girl and Mum's little helper. I did not mind too much the loneliness, neither did I pay much attention to the mild teasing at school about my looks and name, as long as I knew that at home, there was a place for me, my special place as Mum's cherished only girl. Home was where my heart was.

During the rest of my teenage years, there was no longer a good place to be. Along with growing breasts had come periods that I was not prepared for, but they were quickly responded to by Mum with a pack of sanitary pads and 'remember well what I told you about men from now on', a comment the significance of which I had failed to understand for at least a couple more years until I got the connection between the monthly blood and sex and babies in a well taught biology class at school.

As though all of this was not trouble enough, my hair had turned even darker in my teenage years and the downy hair on my arms and legs was now truly unsightly. I was spared the torture of anyone getting sight of my body during the long winters, where no skin would be exposed to anyone's indiscreet eyes. Since the beginning of secondary school, I had at least learnt to deal with my eyebrows. Plucking them out had now become a routine that, although painful, had at last given me a sense of control. There was something indeed that I could do about my monstrousness. The pain would have felt more bearable, I had always thought, if Mum had taken the time to show me how to trim them, if there had been an understanding companion to my sorrow. Nevertheless, taking action, even if it was in this solitary, hidden way, meant that I could at least go to school feeling somewhat protected from shame.

The summers, though, were another business altogether; when my exposed hairy legs and arms poked out of the compulsory summer uniform, I felt constantly embarrassed and self-conscious beyond belief. It did not matter that hardly any of my peers paid any attention to me at school. Alison was now one of the most popular girls in our year, and she discreetly avoided me when we crossed paths in the school corridor. We never sat together any more of course. My repeated and well-rehearsed indifference to being friendless had left me to occupy the familiar space that I had always deep down preferred, that of being invisible. Yet, despite the apparent invisibility that I had managed to achieve, there was nothing that would reassure me enough about exposing my bare limbs.

As for my place at home, it had not remained unchallenged. I still remember with fondness how when I was a little girl, I had held passionately to the conviction that I was the only one that could make Mum happy; The only one that knew how to love Mum the way she needed to be loved. In adolescence, I had not really lost my place as Mum's helper. If anything, Mum would seek me out even more, not only as a helper, but also as the eager listener of more and more stories from her childhood as well as her bitter monologues about Dad's long list of failures and offences. It's just that since that early autumn afternoon of her disclosure, I lost my childish conviction that I could ever make Mum truly happy. So, Mum's unhappiness would now be further proof of my inherent monstrousness that no epilation strategy could ever do enough to alleviate.

The ham and cheese sandwich

> How do children experience the death of a parent, especially in adolescence when they begin developing their gendered identity? Grief is a pervasive feeling that, contrary to popular belief, can accompany us for life. When grief is traumatic though through sudden loss that cannot be put into words or processed, there is the risk of internalising it as a sense of one's own 'badness' through having been implicated or even having 'caused' a parent's death. As in the previous story, here the beginning of adolescence is marked by trauma, this time through tragic loss. Perhaps, one is also left with the question of how human beings can cope with loss, when it feels both unbearable and unrecoverable.

The day it happened, Dad made me a ham and cheese sandwich in the morning. Now he had retired from his job of hygiene inspector for the numerous and expanding cafés and restaurants in our wannabe trendy town, he seemed to invest his considerable energy in sourcing the best ingredients for my lunchbox. Sometimes, I wished I was not an only child, his only son, so that there could be less focus on me, as much as, I have to admit, I loved our one-to-one excursions. They made me feel grown up.

It was less than three months since I had started secondary school, and as any other boy my age would know, blending in, not attracting attention to myself, and especially negative attention, was more than half of the art of surviving impending teenage gloom. I feared I had already most certainly failed on the non-attention grounds by virtue of being left-handed and exceptionally good at maths. But having a lunchbox, when everybody else picked a cheese pie from the canteen in the long break, was just out of the question.

The only problem with telling Dad not to bother with the lunchbox was that the rules and art of not attracting attention applied equally at home. Were I to say to my parents that I did not want a lunchbox, as nobody else had one and everyone had pocket money to buy snacks from the canteen, I would almost certainly get to hear a lecture on the hygienic dangers of eating any food from the canteen, rather surprisingly not as much from Dad, but from Mum who was the lecture person in the family. So, some days, I would remember to open the lunchbox and chew some of the sandwich along with the now slowly liquefying tomatoes cut in quarters and placed next to the foil-wrapped sandwich in a small plastic box, before directly disposing of the rest in the nearby bin, making sure the foil remained in my lunchbox as evidence that the contents had been consumed. Mum was in fact not averse to food being thrown away, as she frequently did this herself, her favourite saying being 'best to throw it in the bin than in our stomachs', but she was almost certain to find fault with whatever I did, be it eating or not eating regardless.

With Dad, it was a different question. He would almost certainly be hurt if he found out that his sandwiches were going in the bin, and probably not do much to show me anyway. The problem though was that he would just not get it, how shameful it was for a boy my age to be noticed as different from the rest, and how, as things stood, I could not help but be different in every single way. The only escape from that was to blend in with the walls like a chameleon and persuade everybody that I was not there at all, for most of the time at least. Unfortunately, Dad was too old to remember his school years, and as much as I loved spending time with him, I couldn't help but wonder sometimes if Dad was too old to remember what it was like to be a child at all.

The secondary school transition was a relatively smooth business, as most of my classmates went along with me to the same state secondary, transferring from our primary school just further down the same little pedestrian street right at the centre of the shopping district in Thessaloniki. Iktinou Street is known for its posh cafés and bars. In primary school, I found the crowd attracted to the cafés a plain inconvenience, as I had to navigate between smoking customers when walking back home. But at the beginning of secondary school, I noticed that some of the coolest kids in class (and I know for a fact that I am not one of them, not that I care that much about it anyway) were already preparing their way from café to bar to disco, sitting on the freshly painted white benches of the café just outside the school, toying with the sugar box until they were playfully shooed away by the owner, who was by now quite accustomed to them.

The transition to secondary school had not been smooth at home though. Mum and Dad had increasingly loud debates about whether their only son, as they put it, confirmed genius already according to both, should go state or private. Mum had insisted and insisted that I sit the exams of the American college, the best-known private in town, and much to my dismay I had indeed come second, which meant that a partial scholarship was offered to me to study there. This upped the game between my parents from debate to screaming arguments, banging the table on both sides as they were still sat across from each other like opposing football teams, after they had sent me to do homework at my desk. What did they even mean, homework? Had they forgotten it was the summer after all? Oh and by the way, in all this, they had forgotten to ask me what I wanted. Hmm, not sure about that anyway, but Dad's side sounded more like he wanted me to be normal, while Mum was preparing me for Harvard already.

In fact, Dad and I had the most intriguing outing in town the other day, when over garlicky meatballs with mustard sauce in the only restaurant that had won

28 The ham and cheese sandwich

five stars under his inspection, Dad drew a strange shape on a napkin that looked like a flower that had lost its petals. I thought the next thing coming was a test in geometry and whether I could manage the same level as university graduates, but instead Dad said:

> 'This is a drawing of a woman's fanny. It is a drawing of a vagina, to be exact. You are old enough to use proper words now.'

I felt speechless, hot sweat coming over my face like I had recently felt in the morning when discovering a hard willy under my linen blanket when I woke up. I tried hard not to giggle. I knew Dad wanted me to be a grown-up since he sent me off to scout school when I was seven patting me on the shoulder telling me that I would now learn to be hardy like a man. I had sensed then that Dad wanted me to be a man very fast, so that we could hang out together, and so that I would always remember my outings with him.

In fact, Dad had told me so once. He had never met either of his parents himself, being by far the youngest in the family with grown-up sisters, his mother's pregnancy an obscene accident when she was convinced she was well past childbearing age. His father died soon after his conception fighting in the First World War, and his mother did not survive his birth. So not only did he grow up being called an 'orphan' but also, despite his sisters' fondness for him, as they had now rather unexpectedly acquired a baby without the complications and restrictions of arranged marriage in their small mountain village, he had to deal for all his life with his older brother's hatred. His brother was only just about a teenager when their mother perished trying to bring him into the world, and his existence was what his brother blamed for his loss. 'I hope you don't become an orphan too, if I die soon', Dad had told me bitterly after one of the increasingly loud arguments my parents had this summer. I understood that to mean, that if Dad died, Mum would most certainly choose to dispose of me in an orphanage like the grey stone building on the outskirts of town we often drove past that always sent a shiver down my spine.

'See the round button at the top?' Dad drew my attention again to the drawing. 'It is called a clitoris. This is where you need to touch a woman gently. You will make her melt with pleasure and she will be yours for ever.'

Later on, when we bought baklava to take home with us to complete a summer's day of treats, I wondered how come, if Dad knew how to make Mum melt with pleasure, she always found reasons to scorn us both, making sure we were both told what she wanted and how she was not getting it. At least the contest over which secondary school I should go to was settled soon after the vagina-drawing day in favour of Dad who insisted that location-wise it made sense to go to the local state school, where many of the middle-class families living in this privileged part of town sent their children, and that we could invest some of the money we would otherwise spend competing for trendy brands of teenage clothes that all kids wore in the American school in advanced lessons in English, which would secure me a place in a top British or American university as soon as I finished high school.

The day it happened was the first time I had buttoned up my coat this year. The early December wind made my ears feel numb as I was turning from Iktinou to Tsimski Street taking a more interesting detour home this time. My latest hobby was counting the squares on the pavement all the way home, and I had just noticed that the squares on Tsimiski Street were completely uninterrupted all the way, and so I could play another favourite game, which was to make sure that I always stood in the middle of each square and that I never stepped on its edge. I avoided the next thought that if I accidentally stepped on the separating line between squares something bad was going to happen, putting it down to the fact I had skipped both breakfast and lunch today and that as much as I preferred to pack all my food intake into the later hours of the day after school time, running on empty for all these hours had made me somewhat grumpy.

When the lift arrived on the second floor, front door key ready in my hand, my aunt popped out of their flat next door, smiling and inviting me in to taste her spaghetti bolognese, which was magically piled high on my plate before I could say 'huh!' This was indeed my absolutely favourite dish, especially the way my aunt made it. I cleared it in less than five minutes and after an honest effort at seconds, I was more than happy to have a deep and restful siesta on the living room couch in front of the flickering images on TV. Mum would have never let me sleep in front of the TV, let alone devour a piece of dark and juicy chocolate cake upon waking, using mostly my fingers. It was only when the woman in question, Mum, arrived later on that day, looking pale and drawn in the face and telling me that Dad had been feeling unwell with a tummy ache and had been taken to hospital, just to make sure that he will get better soon, and that I would have to stay at my aunt's for a few days, as she would spend her time at hospital helping him out, that I suddenly and for no reason at all remembered the well lined-up squares in Tsimiski Street and how well I had done not to step on the lines, other than only one time, just before I was about to turn to my street, when losing my balance, my right foot landed hard on the thick, deep and dust-filled line. I had to persuade myself that it didn't matter quite as much, as right was not my dominant side.

It was three days later when Mum dropped by to pick me up from my aunt's straight after I had finished my lunch. Her platinum blonde hair was shiny against the all black she wore throughout. But the first thing that I noticed really was her eyes, bright red, with pink shadowy bits at the top of the eyelids and little sacks of darker pink, like the skin of a medusa, under the eyes.

'Nicholas, your father died from a heart attack three days ago', she said in a very, very dry voice. 'We have had the funeral this morning. It is all over. It will be the two of us from now on.' Her voice cracked right at the end of the last sentence, but she soon turned her back to me, picking up my things spread over my aunt's living room, while I stayed completely still staring at her.

Later on that evening, in my cold and damp bedroom which was not getting any warmer despite Mum having switched on and bled all the radiators, was the first time I opened my school bag since the day my aunt had invited me into her flat for spaghetti bolognese. The first thing that struck me as I did was the smell, like alcohol turning sour and vinegary. Then, I noticed some grease on the blue underside of my well-lined and insulated new bag, its purchase at the end of last summer marking the beginning of secondary school. As I pulled out my book of Greek literature, and then, the chemistry notebook, I found the aluminium square lying neatly between them. On the last day of my dad's life, I had managed to forget that he had prepared a ham and cheese sandwich for me again with the best ingredients he could source in the market. I passed the crumpled foil square from one hand to the other a few times before getting up to dispose of it in the bin by the kitchen door. It was only after I let go of it that the tears started flowing and rolling, and then there was no end to them.

Awakening

> One of the key events in adolescence is the emergence of sexuality as well as forming one's sexual identity. This may be much more complex than articulating if one is gay or straight. The very first sexual awakening in adolescence is a life-shattering event, and it is not uncommon that one experiences it as a trauma in a subjective sense. Besides, sexual attraction is not only an expression of love, but also of darker feelings such as a wish to dominate, an expression of hatred, and sometimes, like in this story, of envy. Through a play with lightness and darkness, a narrative unfolds that asks questions about the complexities of female friendship and the threat and excitement of one's first encounter with desire.

Norfolk Sands camp, 1–15 August 2011

Day 1

At last, Yasemin and I have boarded the coach for Norfolk Sands this morning at 6.30 am! We have been waiting for this moment for months. Leaving London for two whole weeks, spending time together and, you know what, there will be boys in the camp too! July in London was so boring, but still way better than Year 9 in Cheltering. At least I had time to surf on Facebook all day long. Bliss! Mum and Dad were at work leaving me chores for the day to get me out of FB, but silly them, I could finish them all in the hour before they got home. Cheltering, as you know, is a school that pretends to be progressive while it isn't. Better to attend nun school like in the olden days than a bunch of girls thrown together just by virtue of their parents liking to pretend they are posh, being secretly indoctrinated every morning by horrid Miss Virgin Head. At least her ridiculous assembly speeches gave Yasemin and me plenty of reasons for some serious giggling throughout the school day. But why am I even talking about Cheltering? We are here in Norfolk Sands, a truly hip camp for teens with the coolest sports and dance classes in England and best of all, real water sports run by true deeply tanned water babes.

As soon as we arrived, we were approached by babe number one, Craig, our camp activities coach. He looked about nineteen, so in theory, dating material. He took Yasemin and me aside and said that he has had a look at our files and he could see that we were both very sporty and really good in dance and gymnastics. He had in fact looked at our files so carefully that he had picked up that Yasemin's point of excellence was modern dance and mine creative gymnastics. He said we needed to meet regularly and come up with a plan as there is this end of camp show or something and the two of us could do a combined show perhaps, but our own individual shows as well. Cool!

I can tell you already that Craig has velvety skin. His arms are lean and muscly and grafted with blue veins and he has gingery blond downy hair all over his body like the fur of a kitten. He also has a very nice smile and wears his sun-kissed hair in a cool ponytail. Of course, I was not surprised that he seemed to focus his sky-blue eyes more on Yasemin than on me. Everyone knows that Yasemin is absolutely, breathtakingly, heartstoppingly stunning. Yasemin's dad is Turkish from Istanbul as you may have guessed from her name, a really nice man and a fun dad too, and her mum is Irish. So, North meets South and East meets West. Yasemin's skin is always naturally tanned, no need for fake tans that leave messy patches and an orange tint on your skin for days on end. Her eyes are like the Med and most importantly, as we are now at the height of the summer, Yasemin has endless model legs that given that we are also out of Cheltering for a good two months, she takes every opportunity of showing off through her cropped hot shorts, tired and torn as they should be. It is not even that she shows them off on purpose. Yasemin is genuinely oblivious to how truly beautiful she is, which makes her even more stunning altogether.

Now, I know that objectively I am not terribly ugly either, but let's face it, my legs are pale and plump no matter how much exercise I subject them to every day. My hair is dead-pan straight and blonde and on the thin side, thank Mum for this, my boobs hardly deserve the two pairs of lacy Wonderbras I bought specifically for this holiday with Yasemin, the two weeks I have been waiting for throughout the year. And then there's all the rest. Yasemin is naturally charming and chatty and friendly and I am all shy, turning red like a lobster all over, if somebody says as much as hello to me. At least I don't have any pimples, while Yasemin has a little bit of acne on her cheeks that she manages to conceal with her rich exotic hair that cascades like a waterfall at night round her face. Well, I score one point there versus the million that she deserves.

Day 3

Man, it is truly sick here! We've been at the camp for one full day only, and we have tried canoeing and surfing already. Craig said, exceptionally, we were allowed to try two water sports in one day, as the sun was truly smiling on us all day long yesterday and it isn't like that every day. This was a warning, I guess, and good that he let us spend most of the day by the sea yesterday, as it's been pouring down cats and dogs this morning. Both Yasemin and I fell in the water when we were trying surfing and it was superfun to be in the deep, riding the waves, even though the sea was ice cold. Yasemin said the Med is a much better sea, it's got to be admitted.

But the biggest fun was in the evening. Yasemin and I took all our clothes out of our rucksacks and we swapped some and tried on the new bras. She brought two as well and, guess what, they are cooler than mine, more teenage chic Calvin Klein style. I overdid it with the lace, trying to make my boobs look more grown up. Anyway, at least on that front Yasemin and I score equally. How do I know? Well, I'm a bit embarrassed to write this, but you are my diary and you need to know all my secrets. As we were looking at each other's clothes and stuff, Yasemin said, 'Can I see your boobs?' We were in this giggly mood, our clothes were all over the tent and all make up and pads and stuff spilled on the floor. This is the other super cool thing about this camp, it is not proper school-like, but truly made for teens to have fun. So friends can share a tent for two or three or four, and Yasemin and I were allowed to share our very own tent for a little bit extra cash that our folks were happy to pay, just as long as they got us off the screens. Oh, I forgot to tell you this, this is the one tough condition on the camp. No screens of any kind, not even phones. Like an electronic detox clinic and stuff.

Anyway, I said, 'No!' and then she said, 'I dare you!' and, 'If you do, I'll show you mine too!' and I said, 'OK, then!', giggling. I have to say, she's got really beautiful breasts, and mine are not bad either, other than we are both very small. But hers look upwards, as though pulled by an invisible string and the most bizarre, interesting, exotic thing of all, though I would never tell her any of that, she's got really dark nipples like two smooth milk chocolate buttons. I never knew those even existed. She even asked me if I liked hers and I said yes, trying not to show how shy I was feeling, and she said mine are truly virginal and teen-like, men would go mad over them. Anyway, enough about boobs!

Day 5

Today was the first day we've been told off by the camp supervisor. Craig popped his head in our tent first thing in the morning and saw all the mess on the floor, and he was trying not to smile and be serious like and he said, 'Anyway, girls, are you ready for rehearsals? I'm going to turn a big blind eye to this mess.' Yasemin was super chatty with him and I thought she was showing off a bit as we were both still in our super hot, see-through baby-dolls and I rushed to hide under my duvet, but she went up to the door to chat with him and I think he felt uncomfortable and rushed to say goodbye and to egg us on to get ready.

I don't know if I am imagining it, but Yasemin has been acting a little bit cool towards me since the boobs incident. She is quite silent sometimes when it is the two of us, and she's been reading her book a lot, which is chilled as I love books and stuff too, and I brought quite a few with me. She said she misses her phone and I thought, secretly, she may be a little homesick.

Anyway, the camp supervisor came unexpectedly to inspect our tent in the afternoon, just as we had got back from activities and we were getting ready for supper. He was furious about the stuff on the floor and he said we needed to tidy up everything and he would inspect again first thing tomorrow morning. He was particularly shocked to see the pads and Yasemin's tampons and the bras on the floor, I think, as I noticed he stared at them. I never thought I would say this after Cheltering, but I wish this camp had some more female staff.

We were rather moody after that tidying up in silence, but then Yasemin switched as though she had pushed the happy button and said, 'Let's go and join the others on the beach.' It is Friday today, and every Friday, we were told, there is a beach party, weather permitting, and hints were dropped about happenings there and stuff, we heard another girl saying they let the babes supervise and they turn a blind eye to things. I was not keen as we have made no friends so far, too busy with activities and chatting with each other. But then Yasemin said, 'Come on, it will be fun', and we went and there were these really sporty boys there playing the guitar and girls and boys sitting round in a circle. They all had cans they drank from, only Coke and ginger beer, I'm afraid, alcohol is strictly off limits on the camp. Even Craig turned up at some point and sat with us. He was in fact next to me and I could see his profile in the dark and I have to say, OMG, he's so handsome! After he left, some of the girls produced roll-ups out of their pockets and they started passing round and I thought it was cigarettes but Yasemin pushed my shoulder and she whispered 'good stuff!' and I panicked as up to now I have never done any drugs, you know, and my parents have been giving me a lecture about the risks, blah, blah! Yasemin did lots, but I only had three puffs as it was going round and I passed after that as my head started turning and I could see all stars in the sky super bright as though they had just been set alight. I coughed the first time, which was embarrassing but I managed to keep my cool after that.

When we went back to the tent, I was feeling rather down, don't know why, but Yasemin said she really needed to dance and she danced and danced in the dark while I was falling in and out of sleep and I think she took all her clothes off as well, even at night she must have slept with nothing on as in the morning she asked me to turn my back to her, so she could get out of bed and she said 'Sorry about yesterday' ever so quietly, but I pretended I had fallen back asleep.

Day 9

Today is possibly the first and only time in my entire life that I have felt so truly proud of myself. All these days in the camp, I have become more confident about my body. We do sports for five to six hours a day and it is truly awesome and the food here, it's got to be said, is really horrid, even worse than in Cheltering, so I'm eating like a bird. So, I have begun to see the muscles in my legs and they tanned even if lightly, and maybe it is the lack of mirrors as well, but I thought, you know what, my legs are not that disgusting after all, so now, I started wearing my hot shorts as well and I can tell I have lost quite a bit of weight as they almost fall off me.

But hey, this is not what I'm proud of. It is to do with Craig (again!). Sorry about the repeat! For all these days, we have been rehearsing for two hours a day with him for the show. It is a serious show in fact of professional standard, and we do it twice, once on the last evening here (weeping already!) and once when parents come to pick us up the following afternoon. It's called 'Norfolk Sands has talent!' So, today at the end of my individual practice he said he wanted a serious word with me. I panicked and thought he'll say I'm out of the show or something, but he said:

'Chloe, do you realise how talented you are in gymnastics?'

I forgot to tell you that for all these days, I have been also practising my programme for one hour on my own, and I don't know if it is all the exercise and stuff, but I could never before imagine that I could reach this level. I mean high jump is not my strength, it will never be, unless I shrink to a size zero or something, but I can easily touch my bum with the back of my head and keep it there as well without feeling a single muscle twitch.

'Don't pull my leg, Craig', I said, and I could feel the blush spreading not only on my face and neck, but down my chest too.

'Why do you have such low faith in yourself, Chloe? Have you ever considered having some counselling?'

'Look,' he said, 'we'll try something new!'

Then, the incredible happened, he took my hand in his!!!!!!!!

'Please, look me in the eye, Chloe', he said, stressing his every word.

I did, and as I did, I literally thought I was losing myself into a deep blue sea.

'I have been working in this camp for five years. For all these years, I have hardly come across talent like yours. Some of the stuff you do is near Olympic level. When you leave here, I want you to talk to your parents about taking this further, do you understand? I will also write a report with recommendations. I want you to do your full programme for the show, no cuts. We will manage to accommodate it all.'

When I was leaving, he apologised for holding my hand like that. He did it, he said, so that I could remember what he said for long enough to have to act on it.

Later on, we replayed this scene several times with Yasemin. She role-played Craig holding my hand, but giggling every time before we finished the dialogue.

Day 12

Today is a big, big day! It's the last day of rehearsals before the show tomorrow and it's also the beach party day and, though we woke up in cloudland, it is meant to cheer up and be sunny later on. Yasemin is super excited about the beach party, I know. At supper time she's been all chats and whispers with Dan and Ellie and the rest of them from the joint-smoking group. I think they've been planning to bring some more stuff as last party of the season etc.

To be honest, I'm much more excited about the show. I have doubled my individual rehearsals and I feel I know my programme so well that it gets replayed several times in my sleep every night. It is quite sick! I've got to this point where I can do it on automatic. I've noticed too that Craig is proud of me. I can tell from the way he approves at the end of my rehearsals with him, not too many words, but his eyes are shiny. Do you think I make him happy??? As for Yasemin, she's been really grand. She even offered to drop her dance show to accommodate my full programme, but Craig said, no need, all can fit. A true friend!

Day 13, 8am

Last night proved to be a big night as expected, and I can honestly say this night has been the biggest of my whole entire life. The beach party was fun and you could tell from the beginning there would be happenings and stuff. Even I was less shy and I danced and chatted with some of the boys and, you know what, when Craig came to supervise, I took him to the floor and I danced with him. All innocent and stuff, but OK he may not be nineteen as I was hoping for, but he's only twenty-four, a young lad still, just ten years older than me. He could not even be my dad, could he?

Anyway, I had promised myself not to smoke any puff, as show day today, but hey, there was such a good vibe and we all did a bit in the turning a blind eye window we had when no staff was there and I did not mind as much that all the stars got super shiny again, and this time, I thought how beautiful they were. We also played *kiss or tell* as we were all so high by the end. Basically, we sat in a circle and turned a bottle round and whoever the bottle pointed at, they had to either tell a secret or kiss the person across from them, but a real kiss and stuff. Guess what? When the bottle pointed at Yasemin, we were sitting across from each other and she looked at me and said, 'kiss'. Her eyes had a dark shadow on them, like the sea at midnight. I started giggling of course, and she got on her knees, leant forward and held me by the nape of my neck and . . . and . . . she gave me a real kiss, tongue touching and everything. I could hear everyone cheering, but all I could feel was my knees that had gone like water, all wobbly and stuff and her full lips on mine, I felt them there for hours to come.

Next thing I knew, we were in our tent and I was fast asleep, but a strange, sweet sound brought me round, and I took a quick glance at my alarm clock, 4.03 am it read. To start with, I thought we had a kitten in the tent, as it was that kind of sound, weeping like cats at night some times, but then I got more awake, I worked it out that it was Yasemin crying her eyes out.

'Are you all right?' I whispered.

'No', she said and she sounded full of snot.

'What's wrong?'

She would not speak for a while and then, she said, 'can I come to your bed?' in a very little voice. I really felt for her and to start with she lay there weeping and I patted her head. She told me about her mum. I had no idea! Apparently, she got hospitalised in Ireland for nearly a year with some kind of serious depression and stuff. I knew her mum had been away for a while, but thought she was visiting family, but she said no, her mum had not been right for years, always fighting with her dad that it was all his fault that he made her lose contact with family through marrying a Muslim and stuff.

Anyway, after a while she turned on her side, she had stopped weeping by then, and don't know how it happened, but we started kissing again, and then it was pretty obvious, man, that she knew lots of stuff, 'you won't forget this night', she murmured and . . . and . . . anyway, I won't get into the details as too private and stuff, but basically, I had the big O for the first time ever! And not only once either, as once she got me there one way, she showed me other ways and almost taught me how to achieve it myself and stuff, the insides of my legs are still shaking like a permanent tremor has installed itself there. She said she's been having Os since she was eight, but I find this hard to believe, although she clearly knew her stuff.

She stayed in my bed till 7 and she touched me there several times, different ways and we kissed so much that our lips were sore and swollen. Then, she said, better she goes back to her bed, in case anyone popped in. It felt like my body lost its other half.

Day 14

It's all over. To start with yesterday, I pretended to be unwell to give breakfast a miss and gather myself. I'm not bothered by the 'am I a lesbian now?' stuff, as I think it's stupid to put people into boxes like that anyway, but I thought Yasemin was a friend and I just had an earth-shattering experience with her so I was confused. But then, as it happened, I started shivering a lot, so much so, that I could hardly get out of bed. I put something on and I went to find Craig and as soon as he saw me he sent me straight to the nurse. I mumbled, I was sure it was not a cold, and I was fine and did not want to miss the show and stuff, but I had a fever of 102 °F, basically, you could boil an egg on me. I could tell they got a bit worried as well, as no other signs of illness, as the nurse murmured, for a fever that high. I was sent to spend the last day in bed with paracetamol. I was reading my books, praying the fever would come down, as really, other than that, I was feeling completely well, no sore throat or bad tummy or anything, though I could not do food at all, but I think this was because of all the other turmoil. The nurse said as long as I kept hydrated, it was fine not to eat and she would come and check on me in the afternoon after paracetamol took effect.

Yasemin popped in a few times. She seemed all excited telling me it was mayhem in the camp with all last minute rehearsals and everyone was full of nerves, and then, leaving in a rush, after patting me on the head, 'You poor thing', kind of thing. Was I asking for too much, hoping that she would stay a bit with me or ask me if I was upset I may miss the show? And no kisses either . . . Craig popped in once as well, and he seemed sad and said he would pop in again after the nurse had visited. I tried to read and read, but I was feeling dizzy and must have dozed off several times dreaming invariably of my show and Yasemin's lips on mine.

The nurse came at 4 pm, show planned for 6.30. No change at all. The fever had not gone down, if anything a touch up. She said she would combine now paracetamol with ibuprofen. She said, in all honesty, I'd better stay in bed. After she left, I cried my eyes out, not sure what I was crying about either, but the feeling was that nobody gave a toss about me. By the time Craig popped in at 5.30, I had made up my mind. He asked half-heartedly and I said, no, I was not well enough . . .

As soon as the clock ticked 6.30, it was like magic, I could feel the fever coming down, and I just sweated it all out. Last time I had seen Yasemin was at 4.30 straight after the nurse left. She had said she would come to check on me before the show, but she did not come back. I could tell something was up as she picked all her dance clothes from the tent, her make-up too, and she left without making eye contact.

At 7.15 exactly, the time of my planned gymnastics show, I stood feverless and fully dressed in my gymnastics show gear behind the stage, in the semi-dark shade of the tall birch tree. Craig and Yasemin were at the back of the stage, their backs turned to me, shoulders touching, whispering to each other. She looked truly stunning, deep pink and purple bodice and a cropped satin black skirt falling like water round her long tanned legs, smooth, dark-wood hair gathered like silk in a high tail, full, ruby red lips, almond shaped pearls for eyes. As Craig gave her a light push she swam to the stage, dancing, her steps intercepted by some gracious gymnastics poses that I did not know she was able to do, taken from my planned gymnastics show. As she brought her impeccable performance to a climax after a stunning twenty-five minutes of it, more than twice the length of her previously allocated time, I could hear the audience clapping like firecrackers in the dark and I could see her lean silhouette walking back to Craig, giving him a tight hug. I am still wondering if at that moment of looking behind the stage, she could make out my shadow beside the birch tree.

London in August, or Serendipity

> This story is structurally different from the previous ones in this section, as the narrator is an adult, a practising therapist. Through repeated flashbacks, the story unfolds between the past and the present. Again, the focus here is female friendship and how sexuality can constitute the dark horse at the heart of a falling-out, especially in adolescence. Another theme here is one's encounter with death in adult life and the subjective proximity and fluidity between a past and a present self. The possibility of true affection between women is explored in this story, and such affection, and its inevitable association with the longing for a loving and containing mother, is linked with the beginning of healing one's wounds and finding hope again.

You were the cool, sexy girl that all the boys daydreamed about. You displayed your curves with gusto, and your rich long chocolate brown mane followed you in waving motion. I was excited when I realised you wanted to be best friends. A little bit intimidated too. What did you see in me? Looking back, I think it is sad that I did not see how beautiful you were back then, obsessed as I was with thinness and being a fan of gaunt-looking models. Still, I was in awe of your apparent ease with your body, all curves in just the right places.

When I bumped into you on that breezy and sunny mid-August morning, I did not stop for a second. The thought did not even cross my mind that I had seen you before, that your face looked familiar in some way. Then you called my name, and when I did not respond, gave name and surname pronounced clearly one after another just like in high school. It made me stop in my tracks. Shock made me wave the neatly folded piece of paper I had just received, with my formal diagnosis clearly written in bold, at your face, before quickly realising what I was holding and shoving it back in my bag. Did you notice, I wonder, how my hand shook when I did?

You had gone all the way. Few of us had back then, and I certainly was not one of them, not that I was entirely innocent in that department either. You had taken me under your wing, assuming my innocence was all-encompassing. When you finally introduced me to your boyfriend, well into his twenties and possessing a fast car, a trophy boyfriend for a high school girl, I had to admit, I wondered if it were you or I who needed protection the most. I still remember the bar he took us to, full of oriental opulence, the air thick with perfume and something else that I could not name back then, but now I would call lust. Couples were kissing intertwined on many of the low-lying smooth velvet sofas. The drinks he bought us were intense and aromatic and of unknown origin. He seemed to think that you were his possession, not only through the heavy hand he lay on your shoulder, but also how he interrupted you and corrected what you were saying every time you opened your mouth. Your boyfriend was scary, I decided that night. I did not like the way he glared at you, or at me for that matter. So, when you came to school one day wearing diva black sunglasses badly concealing a bruised eye, I just did not believe you that you had fallen down the stairs. Nobody else seemed to notice though.

It is not all together surprising that I did not recognise you at all that August day. Your luscious, long light-brown hair had been replaced with short white-blonde fluff enveloping elegantly your head like cat fur. You had not lost your seductive looks, not at all, but it was sleekness that was the vehicle for their expression now, and something else that I could not place my finger on. I noticed your red lipstick, perfectly applied like you always had at school, and I felt your eyes falling on me. 'You look great,' you said, 'fresh and innocent like at school. In fact, you have not changed at all, which is why I recognised you straight away!' It is always nice to be told that you look just like you did at seventeen thirty years on, but the irony did not escape me how often in life beginnings and endings seem to come together. Meeting the beginning of adult life just when it is reaching its end.

I was chuffed to hang out with you in the last year of high school, as it gave me access to the cool and slightly naughty group who gathered in the covered part of the courtyard near the toilets to smoke and flirt. Not that I was unpopular before, just a bit shy. We were all in Levi's denim and Timberland or Doc Martens boots, all apart from you. You did not try to keep it a secret that your parents were poor, and I admired you for your honesty; That, and how you managed to be part of the in group without needing the brands as your ticket to coolness.

It must have been serendipity that brought us together that August Saturday morning. As all my friends and family know, I am never in London in August, as I am not fond of the British summer weather. Who is? You had never visited London before, you said. And so, this was your chance to take a careful look at all the designer shops on Marylebone High Street. You were a furniture designer, you said, and this helped me locate the sharp sleekness of your neatly lined coat, brought to life by a multicoloured wrinkled-up silk scarf. I don't like it when people wear their professional identity in too obvious a way, but as always with you, your personality shone through no matter what.

The first time I noticed the green monster rearing its ugly head between us was when I invited you over to my house. We soon spent hours in my room going through what you called my 'treasure boxes', all loaded with stacks of make-up and facial cream samples as well as some jewellery. I never let you leave my house without some trophy to take back with you, and I could see how this must have bore on you. Little did you know how desperate I was to get rid of my little possessions. 'Presents from some relatives in Athens', I told you. At that point in my life, I had not had any therapy yet, and I could just not handle telling anybody that my mother had decided to move to Athens with her lover, that our relationship consisted of half-read cards she sent me regularly enough, neatly placed in fragrant parcels filled with all the little samples she collected from the multi-storey fancy department store where she worked. 'One day, you must come and visit us', she would say, but this day never came along with a specific invite.

I was secretly pleased that you thought I still looked like the girl who was briefly your best friend at seventeen. Later on, when we finally sat at a nearby café with steaming cups of coffee in our hands, I told you I was a therapist. You were surprised. You always imagined therapists to be old and grave-looking, you said. Your comment made me giggle. An instant reminder of how much fun we had together at high school, how few reasons for laughing carelessly I had right now.

It was in your nature to be generous, and so you often invited me back to your flat, where you produced yummy pasta bakes out of the oven. It was one of the few times I would let my guard down with food. 'I didn't know you could eat that much', you would say, smiling, pleased that your nurturing skills were being responded to with grace. You were in charge of the household most of the time, as your parents worked out of town and left for work before dawn. Operating the hoover and the washing machine, but all the other manual skills of housework too were all within your dexterity. We both suffered from empty houses, yours coming alive through your own creative light, mine steeped in my father's melancholy, and the half-hearted efforts of the dry housekeeper he had employed since my mum's departure two years ago. Teenagers love empty houses, but ironically only when they are full most of the time.

You left your girlfriend sleeping in the hotel, you said, and you had a good couple of hours on your hands. She was a nervous flyer and had not managed any sleep during the late night flight you had caught from Athens, where you now lived. Had you just said *girlfriend*? And did I hear it right that you went out of your way to stress what the nature of your relationship was with her? As for me, I did not tell you, at least not while we were still standing up on the wide pavement of the busy high street, that I had also left my husband and two teenage children asleep at home, as though not including them in this visit to the consultant on Harley Street would spare them the consequences of the diagnosis I had just received.

The falling-out was abrupt between us. Like two tiny boats being dropped down a waterfall, the force of water setting them in different directions for ever. Neither of us knew for all these years whether the other's boat survived the drop. The most painful thing was, back then, and even now, thinking about it, that neither of us could see the falling-out coming, not before the last twenty-four hours during which we were still friends.

'You know I have not contemplated becoming a therapist, but I have helped with developing some therapy work in Athens, and I have had some analysis myself', you said quietly when you sat across from me at the cosy round table by the window, a sunray lighting the sugar granules decorating its surface, a reminder of the customers sitting here just before us.

'Really?' I said.

'Yes. The centre I founded along with some other women artists is called "the Shelter", not such an original name, but fit for its purpose. We provide therapy, but also residential services.'

'The Shelter?' I mumbled, feeling like you expected me to understand what you meant; and then it clicked.

It was the end of high school and my father had finally relented and given me the keys of our seaside house, the place where once upon a time we spent happy summers as a family, still full of my childhood toys and teddy bears. I don't know whether it was his inability to face the loss that kept him renting it out for most of the time or his reluctance to let go of me, another woman on the brink of abandoning him, or both. In any case, after I studied so hard for the exams that even he noticed my weight loss and started worrying, after I passed with glowing colours to study for the degree of my choice at the other end of the country, exactly as planned, after my winter paleness outweighed the bleak dark walls of our insufficiently lit home, he offered me the keys, saying 'Here, I have already rented the house from July, but while it's still empty, you can take your friends there and have fun.' It is one of the few moments of generosity I remember over the years coming from my father, but even more importantly, one of the moments that his gaze fell on me. 'Go sunbathing', he said. 'The sun will do you good', as though the sun would provide the warmth lacking in my home with him.

I gasped when you told me how he used to hit you for years, but even worse, how he used to follow you and threaten you, how you could never go anywhere without being in a state of paralysing fear. It took an injunction order, you said, to stop him, and even then, years later, he called you, asking you if you wanted to marry him.

'Was it your father arranging the injunction?' I asked naively.

You laughed as though you were genuinely amused. 'You are kidding me, right? Dad used to plead with him to excuse my bad behaviour. He was in awe of his wealth; that a rich boy was after his daughter. He just did not get it why I did not want to marry him.'

It was an aunt of yours, you told me, in whose office you worked for your first summer job, who got concerned. She arranged everything for you as well as helping you apply for a degree. She helped you get your life together. You will always be grateful to her, you said.

'It feels great to be able to help other women in similar situations through founding "the Shelter". It feels even better than getting the help for myself, though that help was desperately needed', you said.

When I first bumped into you on the high street, I thought we had nothing in common. Now, I could see that I was plainly wrong.

Thinking about it, our lives had diverted even before that fateful week by the sea. Your life was arrested by your boyfriend, mine had sped over since I went out with the boy I had just begun to date; head over heels with him I was. You took to freedom like an animal held in captivity for far too long. Our plan was solid, we got a lift before dawn by the dad of a common friend who was joining us for the week. For the first time in a long while, your boyfriend did not know where you were. And all you wanted to do with your freedom was go wild, meet other boys, take them to bed. Was this what you needed to feel free? Were you being like my mum? Exchanging one kind of slavery for the next? For the first time since you wanted to be friends, I was no longer in awe of you.

Sitting at the round table by the window, it felt like we had met yesterday. There was no awkwardness, no pause at all. Only the trepidation I felt deep in my stomach about what my life would look like to the friend I had not seen for the last thirty years. Would it measure up? We had both gone places in life, it was obvious from the beginning. This was enough. So, when you had finished your story about how you found in your girlfriend another kind of shelter from men, from all your relationships before that you had found so destructive, I did not hesitate to take my turn. You were astonished to hear that I was still with the same boyfriend I had met back then at seventeen, and this had made my life very smooth in some ways, and in others not. You asked after my children, their names, their ages, and your smile was genuinely sweet when you stared at their pictures. I secretly felt sad for you that you had settled for childlessness, but I knew in my gut that you had found the right place for you.

'I want you to leave my house and not come back', I told you firmly. You looked at me very intensely, and then you quietly closed the door behind you, not turning back. We never exchanged a word since then, not till today. You had dragged us in the middle of an unbearably hot, but still luminous early evening to go meet these boys you knew, who were camping nearby. Jenni and I barely knew them at all, as they were from a neighbouring high school, but you always had it in you to attract boys like bees in a beehive. It took walking for long on the blazingly hot motorway, nearly getting run over, then having to hitchhike and get dropped in the middle of nowhere, when the guy established that none of us were interested in having sex with him. Then, walking some more in the dusk. It felt dangerous, life-threatening almost, you got high on risk. We spent the night with the boys, who were kind enough to let Jenni and me sleep in their tent. We didn't see you all night, you were swallowed up, like a sheep in the midst of a pack of wolves. The next day you were on a high and you reluctantly came back with us. This time, we could thankfully take a public bus back. The atmosphere was icy between us. Few words were exchanged, despite going for a swim and sunbathing, all three of us topless next to each other. We laughed about the peasant man who had given us a lift, his accent and nasty looks, but the fear had still not left my bones.

'I am not well', I mumbled, and my eyes got tearful, before I could reverse the flow.

You looked at me, in this way only close girlfriends can. You held my hand.

'What's wrong?' you whispered.

'Inoperable brain tumour. Apparently, I am lucky (lucky?), it won't affect my cognitive function, but it will make me sick, unbearably dizzy, kill me of course in the end.'

'What will you do?'

'What can I do?' I laughed.

'There is always something one can do.'

'I had thought it was psychosomatic, the therapist in me. I wish it was. Just wanted to be around for my children, you know.'

'You must, you will.'

You had a way of saying things that would irritate the hell out of me if uttered by anybody else, and yet, coming from you, it warmed my heart.

When in the late afternoon, you started packing your rucksack, Jenni and I watched you silently. Then, we saw you pack a serrated knife from the kitchen.

'Where are you off to?' Jenni mumbled, and I could hear dread in her voice.

'I am having a date with one of the boys', you said, as though proud of yourself.

'So, you are going all the way back? Hitchhiking again?'

'I am equipped this time', you smiled.

So, when you were at the door, I told you, I asked you to leave, for ever.

We sat at this café for at least an hour, holding hands. Our eyes were teary. I don't remember everything that was said, but it was as though there was a string between us holding us together. You told me stories about the women you had encountered at the shelter. How many of them were on the brink of death, physically and emotionally as well. I told you about my work, how I rescued women in a more subtle way by helping them discover a good enough mother in them. You said you were truly sad not to have been in my life for all these years. On that, we both cried. I still can't remember much of what was said, and yet, when I left the café, not before exchanging phone numbers, and inviting you with your girlfriend to my house of course, I knew that I was at the beginning of the journey rather than at the end.

Part II

Ellie

> In this collection of seven short stories, the narrator is Ellie, a psychoanalytic psychotherapist in her early forties who runs a private practice in the City of London. We witness Ellie's work with seven different patients, some long-term and some early on in the therapy or in a one-off session. The focus here is on Ellie's subjective experience of each of these patients and her free associations. We also get to know Ellie's own dark side linked with her past and her unresolved relationship with her mother. One of the main themes here is how the therapist's own blind spots and particular difficulties in close relationships can be worked through creatively in each different therapy relationship.

Mess

> One of the issues that has defined psychoanalysis, historically and through its cultural representation in the arts, is the erotic transference. This is often portrayed as a situation where the patient, most often female, falls in love with the therapist, most often older and male. The orthodox psychoanalytic interpretation of such erotic entanglement focuses on unresolved issues from a relationship with a parent which get transferred onto the therapeutic relationship, and which can affect both parties. The more recent relational movement in psychoanalysis has recognised a greater complexity in the emergence of erotic feelings in the therapeutic relationship, often related to early attachment and loss. It also recognises that the therapeutic relationship is real, and complex feelings can emerge, like in any other relationship. The short stories in this and the following part focus on the therapist's private and subjective experience of the therapeutic relationship. Here, questions are posed about the nature of erotic subjectivity, and to what extent it has to be linked with one's gendered identity and sexual orientation or whether it corresponds to a more embodied experience of oneself and the other.

'I'll get straight to the point', she says . . .

I am transfixed by the scent in the room.
It's like jasmine nights in Rome,
Like lemon groves in the South of France,
Like the scent of coconut tropical oil on wet, salty skin just straight after coming out of the water,
Like silky Alphonso mango, its orange, sticky juice getting between my fingers.

She crosses her legs. The shuffling of the soft fabric of her Indian embroidered silk peacock-coloured skirt (Monsoon?) reaches my ears like the rhythmic sound of waves crashing on shell-peppered white sand.

'I have to get straight to the point, one because I have had therapy before, in fact, years and years of it, but mainly because I am in a real mess, and it needs sorting asap, no time to waste at my age, I have no years of youth left to indulge lying on the couch ruminating over the darkness of the world, you see.'

I am fixated by her ring. It forms perfectly arranged ruby petals on her wedding finger. The smoothness of the silky fabric of her clothes, her white long fingers spreading desperately over her eyes now, the undoubtedly Italian make of her velvety ankle boots scratched by the roughness of her voice when she spoke, the urgency of her despair.

I nod quietly. Today is one of the sunniest days of this April so far, although not warm yet. In fact, the early morning frost had settled on my car windows, making it hard to see as I travelled to the tube station, before parking it on the side road as planned and taking the tube to the City, to my new consulting room. Three hours booked this morning, just enough time to park for a full four-hour slot and be back on time to avoid getting a ticket. As she sits comfortably on the dark green velvet chair, the cold morning light falling softly on her impeccable features, I notice her sun-kissed blonde hair, her warm blue eyes, sitting comfortably on dark olive skin, her full lips.

She sighs. 'I'm having an affair', she says. 'And I'm getting married in three months, in July. Not to the person I'm having the affair with of course!'

'Oh!'

'Look, I'm thirty-nine, last chance to have children, to settle, to have the life I want.'

Is it smoke I am detecting in the air? As though she has just lit a post-coital cigarette, inhaling deeply, peering at me impatiently, looking out to me to give her the solution she needs right now.

I clear my throat. Have no idea what to say, but sense I am expected to say something. 'And is this the reason you feel in a mess? Because you are getting married while having an affair at the same time? You think it's time to settle, with the right guy? Perhaps, while having feelings for somebody else?'

'No, I am getting married because I am having feelings for *him*, Greg, my future husband, not somebody else!'

'Right . . .'

'But . . .'

'Hmm?'

In the silence, the scent travels to me again.
I think of squashed limes in a mojito over a Pacific sunset in Santa Monica,
Of vanilla-scented hot milk in a steaming vanilla latte.
I am walking out of the shower barefooted on patterned Moroccan tiles
In my nostrils, the scent of the most gorgeous holiday I have ever been on,
And those I have only dreamt of.
Yet, the scent is discreet enough to make me wonder if there is any in the room at all
Or if it has all been in my mind.

'Where do you come from?' I mumble.

'Pardon?' she says, almost jumping back.

'Do you mind me asking?'

'No. It's just, just that I am hardly ever asked this question, I don't have an accent. Do I?'

God, she is right! What's wrong with me today? Did I think I was strolling on the South Bank, observing the tourists by the London Eye or was it, unwittingly, revenge for still being asked this question in my local Costa while ordering my flat white, after more than twenty years of living here?

'Well, you may be on to something. We finally settled here when I was twelve. My parents met in Sydney where my father was a diplomat for the Italian embassy. After that, they never settled in one place, they had the travelling bug, citizens of the world. Mum followed him around everywhere, she even encouraged him to keep moving. And we moved as well, all the time, me and my little brother I mean, well till I was twelve, then things changed.'

'What made your parents decide to settle?'

'Me, I guess. I needed to go to a good school. I sat a difficult exam, then an interview for a prestigious art school. It was obvious by then I had some inclination to art. And also, my father got a senior post in London that could be long-term for a change.'

'What did your childhood, the moving around feel like?'

'Oh please, don't give me this. I told you already, I had years of therapy. No, I wasn't traumatised by the moving around, no it was not a childhood of broken attachments, poor me lost in the big wide world. It was vibrant and colourful and lively and we all loved it. Honestly!'

She looks outside the window and I can see her fine profile, tiger-like and fierce.

I am sure she does not quite expect it, but I love fierce women.

'Was it the settling then that was difficult?'

'Yes, I would say so. It was like all colour went out of our life. In fact, school was the only good thing for me, I loved it. But my parents' marriage did not survive the move. It was painful to watch.'

'I see.'

'Shall I tell you about the affair then?'

'If you'd like.'

'It's with a colleague from work. It happened over drinks about six months ago. I hadn't even noticed him before. I mean, he's handsome . . . and intelligent, always a winning combination, one of these men who know what they are doing. You know?'

'Hmm . . .'

'So, it was drinks after work, there is a lot of that going on, then somehow everyone left and we lingered. It didn't seem strange at the time, but now I even wonder if other people noticed, not that I care about gossip and the rest.'

'And what happened?'

'Nothing. I mean no sex that time. He leaned over and kissed me over the pub table. I was shocked. Didn't see it coming, but the energy between us was instant, like an electric current hitting me.'

Skin on skin, salty lips, burning sunshine, teenage summer love. Who was I to find pathology in her affair? It sounded as delicious as my hot summers on the island where my granny lived while my parents were too busy with work, the island my mother loved so much. Such freedom and the thrill of being out of sight.

'And what is it like with your boyfriend, I mean future husband?'

'You don't need to correct yourself. It doesn't matter in a way. Does it?'

'Well, in fact, I was wondering about it. I mean when the affair started, you said six months ago, were there plans then to get married?'

She looks out of the window.

That tiger profile; the tanned smooth skin; what would it feel like to touch her?
I recoil.

'Very good point. I'm impressed, if not a little humiliated, that I didn't think of it myself. Greg must have just proposed to me then. I was trying to calculate the dates. It was a warm autumn last year. September, ripe with fruit, lingered into October. September is my favourite month in this country in fact, wet, but warm and sunny, like living in Sydney once again. I remember Greg and I would invite friends to have cocktails on our roof terrace. Late in the evening we would throw shawls around us and watch the lights of the West Hampstead trains passing by. It was magical. There is much good energy between us, we have fights, but good sex too and fun. I would not have said yes otherwise. He proposed on one of these early autumn summer-like evenings. I'm sure the thing with my colleague had not quite started then yet, but it must've done soon after, as I remember it was still not autumnally chilly when we walked out of that pub . . .'

What was her name again? How embarrassing. I was given it of course, along with the referral. Something unusual. Tabitha?

'Funnily enough, you asked about my accent, even though I don't have one, but not about my name. Everyone asks about my name and where it comes from', she said after a while looking straight at me.

Is she seeing right through me, reading all my intimate thoughts?
I blush.

'Tallara is an Australian aboriginal name. My mum has some indigenous roots, just enough to make her look interesting . . .'

'I see. And are you close to your mother?'

'Well, the reason I went to therapy was that, I was close to both of them, but when they started the process of divorce, I hated my father and felt for my mother and was compelled to take sides with her. What I understand from therapy is that I felt too much for her in some way, maybe out of guilt for her suffering, and it was suffocating me.'

'In what way did you feel for her?'

'My father was not exactly monogamous. I think I always kind of knew that. I don't know though that this was much bother to her, not at least when they had fun together, when they were travelling. The problem was when boredom set in.'

'You mean that what destroyed your parents' marriage was not your father's affairs, but when they could no longer have fun together?'

'Yes, absolutely. I could not see that at eighteen when I went to therapy distraught about the divorce, all I could think then was how much I hated my father and how it was all his fault, but then therapy helped me see his side. He was just a high thrill, high intensity man, and my mother was the same, they were good like that together while it worked. Good creative stuff, you see what I mean?'

'So, perhaps your having an affair may be a way to keep the fun in your relationship too. To make sure you don't settle with each other and lose it.'

'Aha! That would make sense. If only it was not so messy. The other man makes claims over me. And as annoying as that is, it's also sexy and confusing . . .' She let out a sigh. 'How long do we have?'

'Five minutes only, I'm afraid. There is a lot to unpack here. We will need to look into some of this next time.'

'I just wanted to say, I am not sure about starting therapy again, although some of what you said was insightful and made me think. I just do not know if I can bear to put myself in the hands of somebody again. Can I think about it? When do you need to know by?'

***

After she left, I opened the window to air the room before my next client. I plumped the cushions on the chair she was sitting in and I could not resist putting my hands gently on them and feeling the warmth her body had left behind. After I had finished my other two sessions, both well attended and ripe with material – a truly productive morning – I found myself lingering near the client's chair where her perfume, as sunny as an Australian day by the beach, reached my nostrils, as delicate and yet as strong as if she was still here. As I put my Monsoon light spring coat on (this is what her peacock skirt reminded me of, it occurred to me now, my gorgeous newly bought embroidered coat), getting ready to pick up the car by the station and meet Luke for a catch-up lunch, before he set off for his business trip tonight, I thought I sensed her smell on my fingers and I was convinced I would be seeing her again. I wondered if Luke would detect a different scent on me too. I prepared mentally to defend myself against any forthcoming accusations of cheating.

At arm's length

This short story is the first one where we see one of the teenagers from Part I in the consulting room as an adult. This offers, I hope, another perspective on how arresting trauma can be, but also on how the past and the present are inherently intertwined. Therapy, in this story, is used as a safeguard against further trauma and loss, but also as a defence against accepting the risks that close relationships and intimacy entail. The story raises questions about the nature of grief and trauma, and whether either can ever be fully overcome. It also hints at the potential parallels in the therapist and patient life trajectories, and how those often constitute the unconscious fabric of their connection.

Dear Ellie,

I am writing this between sessions and I hope that it is OK for you that I communicate in this way. I know it is ridiculous that you are receiving a long letter from me, when you are going to see me in two days, but I have thought about this for some time, and it is the only way I found to tell you what I need to say. I have in fact thought for a long time about terminating therapy, but I know that if I do without letting you know what I need to tell you, it will be yet one more thing to haunt me amongst the ghosts that have brought me to therapy. You may understand why my predicament has made me doubt that therapy is working as it should, or in any case that it has been working for me, as if it did, I would not have to write you a letter to discuss things in the first place . . .

I paused. I placed the letter, mostly unread, on the corner desk by the window of my consulting room, and turning my back to it, I looked outside the window at the outline of the city. It was a gloriously sunny day, the sky fresh and the light crisp, highlighting the Gherkin, the Shard and all the other sharp shapes I loved to stare at between sessions for contemplation. When I checked in early this morning, I had a rare moment of looking over my life and feeling pleased about how things stood, almost proud of myself. Coming to London for a postgrad in psychosocial studies had been a desperate escape from the deadliness of home, but the first years were dreadfully lonely and the culture shock lingered beyond belief. When I had lived in Europe before, even if briefly, as part of an undergrad student exchange, I had taken to cultural diversity with delight. Yet nothing could have prepared me for nineties London, when I first arrived. It was hard to spot any place at all for a decent cup of coffee, and I still remember vividly to this day how my first encounter with Indian food made me double up every time I visited the toilet for days after. I was not easy to make friends, as I have a tendency to conceal shyness with aloofness, so it took quite a while for the dreadful sense of being lost in an alien place to subside. Being with Luke despite lingering doubts about how long it was going to last for, settling down in an apartment with him for the last year, having a small, but established practice of two mornings and two evenings a week in the City, a voluntary placement in the NHS, all this made me feel that my life had started to fall together at last. It was the first time that I felt the boxes were being ticked in the right places and for the right reasons.

I knew I had to overcome my aversion to reading Chloe's letter, but before doing so, I had to deal with my annoyance that on a rare day of reviewing where I was in my life with pleasure, I had received a letter from one of my most settled and not challenging patients that, as she rightly pointed out, meant trouble. If all was well between us, as she was spot-on to remark, she would not be writing me a long letter between sessions. When I had first seen Chloe three years ago, I had significant doubts about whether I was the right therapist for her. She had found me as rather unfortunately many patients do, apparently just on the basis of postcode. She was a manager in a bank nearby. I could see of course that what brought her to therapy was significant trauma and loss, but other than that, her life seemed settled. I still recalled clearly discussing this in supervision, if it was legitimate, that is, for the therapist to be less settled in their life than their patient as well as having a lack of expertise, as I had put it, in the area of her trauma. It didn't help that at the time she came to see me I had just come out of a medium-term relationship in my usual way – a combination of minor disappointments and more major suspicions about the guy's honesty had made me decide that it was easier to stop than to go on. Chloe, on the other hand, was in a stable relationship for over ten years, and she also had a two-year-old, whose picture revealing a spirited, but also angelic-looking little boy had sent flutters to my chest. What brought her to therapy was a horrific and totally unexpected event, a stillbirth.

Chloe had always struck me as a woman of almost abnormally smooth and even temper. This was another area of doubt about my seeing her, as it was almost too tempting to interpret as false what seemed normal for her, and yet totally alien to me – an even temperament. Her relationship was also calm with no explosions of passion, but what seemed to be a genuine, sibling-like connection. Chloe had explained to me that if there was any area of sadness in her life at all before the stillbirth, it had been that both her and her partner, Fergus, were only children. She had readily accepted my interpretation that perhaps they had found a sibling in each other, but this did not take the existential loneliness away, she had said.

Their son was not planned despite both of them being in their late thirties, when his conception became apparent. They were both busy with their careers when it happened, and yet able to accept that it must have not been a complete accident after all. As much as his birth was a shock to their urban way of life, it took away some of the loneliness they both complained about, and as a result, they quickly agreed that it was not right to bring another only child into the world.

'I am not good at succeeding in having the things I really want in life', Chloe had remarked in one of the first sessions with much sadness in her eyes. I still remembered that sentence clearly as it was the very moment I warmed to her, and my doubts about seeing her had dissipated at once. It was indeed, it seemed, one of the few times she had wanted something with passion. She had embarked on a health regime before even trying to conceive, wanting to do things properly this time. And things seemed smooth and easy to start with, as she fell pregnant soon after, and like her previous pregnancy, this one progressed well. This time round, they decided to break with tradition and to find out the baby's sex at twenty weeks. She did not ideally want to have any more than two children, she said, as she was really hoping this one would be a girl. I can only guess that Chloe felt like me when overlooking the city outline under a blue sky this morning, when she discovered that it was a girl indeed. Life smiled at her.

Chloe was thirty-nine when she first came to see me. Exactly as old as I was. She had been through a year of PTSD-focused therapy in the NHS after the stillbirth, when longer-term work was suggested to her, as she remained reluctant to try getting pregnant again despite both her and Fergus still wanting another child. She was told her reluctance might point to some trauma in her past that longer-term analytic therapy would help her connect with, but such trauma had not proven easy to trace. She came from a pair of overworked and slightly preoccupied parents who had decided that having one child was just right for their lifestyle, and whose attention to her was somewhat elliptical, but benign. Chloe had speculated that perhaps paying attention to more than one young child at once was something that she would not know how to fit into her lifestyle either.

Yet, I sensed that the trauma of the stillbirth, and even more so the inexplicability of it, had remained raw despite having done the PTSD-focused therapy, which she often used as a shield against opening the incident up again with me. It was only once during one of the early sessions that she had told me the full story, but it had managed to produce PTSD symptoms in me, as it kept coming to my mind and even turned up in my dreams again and again.

She had woken up one spring morning, she said, about three weeks before she was due with a strange sense that something was wrong. She remembered staying in bed for a while, moving her body gently, trying to see if there were any signs of unusual discomfort or upcoming labour. There were not. She remembered thinking that it was a real luxury to be able to stay in bed like that as not only she had just begun her maternity leave, but Jackson seemed to be sleeping in late. She knew it was late as Fergus had gone to work already and the scent of his aftershave lingered pleasantly in the semi-dark. As much as both her pregnancies had been smooth, she suffered from the usual exhausting insomnia of the last stages, so it was completely unheard of for her to sleep through like that. She got up to take her mobile off its charger, which confirmed that it was indeed nearly eight o'clock, and she went straight back to bed, having just realised exactly what was wrong. There was no movement. She lay there, hoping that Jackson would take a few more minutes to call for her, doing all her usual tricks to wake the baby up, turning on her side, curling her legs up and then stretching them away, tickling her belly and in the end, poking it in desperation. Nothing. Chloe said that there was a particular moment soon after that which meant no degree of false hope-giving from Fergus or the hospital staff later on could dissuade her from the quiet knowledge of the horrendous reality. Her baby girl had died.

The rest was a frenzy. Fergus came back from work. They took Jackson to his childminder. They checked into the hospital. Two different scans. There is no heartbeat, the sonographer confirmed. I am sorry. How many people had told her 'I am sorry' in one hour? Then, an induction. Calling her mum to pick up Jackson. Asking her to take him home with her. She needed the night, they needed the night by themselves. The labour was awful. A true slaughter. She had remained calm throughout, secretly wishing that she would die as well. She knew she could not face up to the time after. The baby was beautiful. She could see Fergus in her strawberry-shaped lips, the dark hair. She could not feel much when holding her. The hysteria came after, when she was taken away. She kept screaming 'why?'. She was taken to a private room. She still demanded that she got an answer. Fergus held her to start with while she screamed. Then, he left abruptly. 'Had to get some fresh air', he said when he came back fifteen minutes later. But why? This was what still bothered her. They could not tell. The foetus seemed to have been deprived of oxygen. It wasn't clear why. Perhaps she had unwittingly compressed something in her sleep. Had she smothered her own baby?

She suffered from unexplained high fevers for weeks after. Every other day she was told to rush to the A & E as the midwife who followed her through would get alarmed, thinking that she was suffering from a postpartum infection. No trace of an infection was ever found. In the end, she learnt not to pay attention. She almost took pleasure in the familiar shivering, the urge to cover herself and then, the eventual cold sweat when the soaring temperature started dropping again.

Their life changed afterwards. She went back to work full-time. Fergus took a year off to do his art, what he always wanted to do. He spent long hours in his studio working on hard materials. Her parents got much more involved with Jackson. They got less. In fact, Fergus took it upon himself to spend a few afternoons with him taking him to the park and to playgroups. She was the least involved. She felt she had to protect him from the dark hole inside.

***

'Can you describe Chloe to me?' my supervisor asked me once. 'Despite all this, she does not come across to me clearly.'

'Do you mean physically?'

'Anything that comes to mind.'

I hesitated. 'She has told me once that she looks stereotypically English, and though I don't know what that is, there is something somewhat unremarkable about her. I mean she is good-looking, but not in a way that would turn heads in the street. She has dark-blonde hair, very straight and long, hazel eyes . . . rather kind eyes. She is slim and well dressed. I always see her in suits as she comes straight from work, but I can tell that she has good taste.' I hesitated again. 'I guess if there is something peculiar about her, it's how she is when she comes into the room and just before she leaves. I can't quite describe it, but at those moments, she comes across as tense. And shy.'

'In what way?'

'As though she is shy to see me or to be seen by me. As though she is trying to discern something about me as well. But then, once she settles into the chair, the shyness goes and what takes over is something much more flat. But when she is up, ready to go again, she sends me this look, something like sadness and, perhaps, something unspoken.'

'Can you take it up with her?'

'I wouldn't know how. It is really vague, just a feeling I get.'

'And how do you feel at those moments?'

'Tense. But then . . . then, I tend to forget about it when she starts speaking.'

***

I had taken Chloe to supervision not that long ago. I had complained that we seemed to have settled into a comfortable routine. Chloe said that she saw therapy as a space that meant that things were still open to change, and yet the fact that she had just turned forty-two and didn't seem concerned that they were not even trying for a baby was rather worrying in itself. I wondered if I was in fact colluding with some foreclosure of the possibility of healing the trauma. Silently, I also wondered if Chloe and I were becoming mirror images of each other. Risk avoidant, keeping life at arm's length. Was I helping her get better or worse?

I picked the letter up again with a new sense of confidence that the clue was somewhere there. Things were stale, they needed to move, to move fast. I scrolled through the beginning that I had read already and my eyes were able to focus at what seemed like exactly the right spot.

> . . . *The thing is, Ellie, that you remind me of somebody from the past, somebody I haven't mentioned. When the PTSD therapist suggested that there may have been a trauma in the past, she, Yasemin, had come to mind and what had happened back then. But then I thought, this is not really trauma and I was somewhat embarrassed to mention it anyway. And then, when I first came to see you, I was not sure that we connected. I mean I was planning to ask you things like, do you have children, can you imagine what it's like to lose one. Then, I saw you and, though you don't really look like her, I mean you hardly look at all like her, but maybe it is the Mediterranean connection or something, but for whatever reason you remind me of her. You come across as self-possessed and confident, but also a bit sad and dark, and all this together is so much like Yasemin.*

I am sorry I know I don't make sense. Yasemin was a friend of mine in high school. We were best friends, but then something happened and I fell in love with her, but in the end it proved to be unrequited. At least, at some point she seemed to want me, but then it all fell apart and it was all confusing and hurtful. In fact, the most hurtful experience of my life after the stillbirth. And the thing is, I know you are my therapist and all that, but I am almost getting these flashbacks of what happened with Yasemin after the sessions, it is like I re-live the night when we made love, my very first time of making love with anybody.

This is why I didn't really want to live after the stillbirth even though I felt I had to for Jackson and Fergus. I just knew after Yasemin that some experiences mark you for life. The hurt never ever goes away even if it fades in intensity. Even Fergus, I think, I was attracted to him to start with because he is one of these men with a strong feminine side and, also, he truly looks like her. She was half-Turkish, half-Irish, and I think they must have some similar Celtic roots. I must have been looking for her ever since.

I also think the PTSD therapist was right. I used to get the same fevers after Yasemin had made love to me and soon after, she stopped talking to me all together. I also used to ask myself why, why should she treat me so cruelly? And like with losing the baby, every time I used to ask the why question I would turn into a hysterical mess . . .

Though of course, my first reaction was to feel stupid and inept, I managed to soon feel excited about what Chloe had shared with me in the letter. I could see that the reason I had not picked up her erotic feelings towards me was that Chloe really needed them to remain hidden. The danger was double. It may be that if I knew about them, I would have been unable to resist them and I would have ended up like Yasemin acting them out. Or even worse, she would soon know that her feelings were not being reciprocated and she would have to abruptly stop the therapy, as she was already thinking of doing, and go away humiliated like she had done in the aftermath of the entanglement with Yasemin, who seemed to have lost all interest in her straight after. I could see that, in investing me with this supposed similarity with Yasemin, and the fact that we were exactly the same age was in a way an uncanny coincidence, Chloe had managed both to remain at a point of false safety, keeping her life at arm's length, but also to invest the therapy with the hope of change. The crucial difference this time was that unlike when Yasemin made an unexpected pass at her and then humiliated her soon after, this time, by keeping her feelings well hidden, Chloe felt that she was in control of regulating feelings that were so intense that threatened to throw her off the precipice at once.

In the sessions that followed, we went through the incident with Yasemin in a summer camp when Chloe was sixteen. Apparently, Chloe was a talented gymnast in her teens, but she lacked the confidence and self-love that would help her see clearly how good she was. Yasemin and Chloe found themselves in competition through trying to get the attention of their young and handsome coach.

After a sleepless night when Yasemin introduced Chloe to the pleasures and darkness of adult love, Chloe missed her final gymnastics show while suffering from an unexplained high fever. Yasemin, on the other hand, performed a double show by herself.

To my surprise, Chloe was resistant to my interpretation that Yasemin acted in envy and greed. After all these years, it still seemed too hurtful to deconstruct the memory of sexual intimacy and to introduce feelings other than love to what seemed like momentary, but unforgettable bliss. What I could help her see though was that what she truly wanted back then was neither Yasemin, nor the handsome coach, nor making love with either of them. What she truly wanted was to gain confidence in her body's ability to perform and excel, to learn how to love herself. We also focused gently on Chloe's relationship with her mother and how her preoccupation with work had made Chloe doubt that she had ever really wanted her. Once again, I came across in her, exactly like in myself, the impossibility of disentangling love for oneself from that ultimate love for and from the mother. Yet, only a few sessions after receiving the letter, it was easy to see that Chloe had started feeling that despite the deadly risks entailed, trying for another baby while she still could may be the closest she could get to beginning to love herself again.

The secret

> Bion's famous statement, that the therapist should enter the room with no memory or desire and the difficulty of doing so, is at the core of this short story. Traditional psychoanalysis has stressed the importance of the therapist's neutrality, yet neutrality is not always experienced as such in the context of the therapeutic relationship. Sometimes, the therapist's professional neutrality can come across as cold and withholding or even cruel. In a relational context, it is increasingly recognised that both parties of the therapeutic relationship are emotionally implicated with each other. As long as this is processed and utilised in the service of the patient, it can be a profoundly formative experience for both. A question raised in this short story is about the therapist's sense of ethics. What is the therapist's position in relation to a patient's decision and choice, especially when matters around life and death can be affected by such a decision?

It was in the middle of a cloudy November morning that I found myself expecting Karen for her fifth session. I'd had a cancellation earlier and I delighted in the opportunity of sipping my black Americano quietly, and finding my thoughts drifting more and more towards her, the closer it got to the session time. At forty-two, I was still considered to be a young therapist and I was mostly referred people who were in their twenties and thirties. Funny how therapists are not seen as mature enough until they reach an age at which most other professionals have well begun their retirement. Karen was fifty-seven, a GP, and from the beginning, she seemed to have received my younger age graciously. That as well as my accent. There were no questions about my years of clinical experience, which were considerable in any case, or where I came from, just a subtle sense of recognition of what it takes to be with people in their pain, a camaraderie perhaps, that she and I both knew what being a clinician meant in the true sense of the word.

It is rare for me to like somebody, patient or not, as much as I liked Karen. We clicked from the first ten minutes of session one. My tendency is to always look for the darkness, for what's underneath, how things will suddenly become complicated after the next bend, always waiting for the crash to happen sooner or later. It is not that Karen was not honest from the beginning in letting me know that there was something difficult to discuss, but that she would take her time with it. She didn't want, she said, to let it take over her sessions, the thing was not her. It was almost as though she had painted in accurate colours that crash I had been expecting to happen for all my life since my mother walked out on us in my teens, the crash that, as my own therapist used to say, had already taken place, and yet, I always expected it to be around the corner. So, it has got to be said that I felt plain stupid that a patient had given me such clear warning that there was something the matter, yet I was sitting comfortably there enjoying her claims that she always wanted to have therapy and what a treat it felt to have finally arrived.

She was confused about her identity, she said. The youngest of four children, her mother's deep Irishness had felt like a dirty secret her father wanted to get rid of, and yet, it was precisely what had felt mostly good about her mother, she was warm and tactile and chatty, open like a green field leading into the ocean. Both her parents were doctors, her father a surgeon and her mum a GP choosing to work in an ethnically mixed inner city London postcode. It was as though her parents increasingly wore their class differences like shields preparing for war: her dad his boarding school upbringing and her mum her childhood of freedom and neglect in rural Ireland. Her mum moved out to study medicine when the freedom started wearing out and her emerging sexuality and Catholicism caught up with her. Divorces are traumatic for children, Karen had remarked, but parents staying together for obscure reasons may be more so, don't you think? She felt that she had always wanted to explore that in therapy; she had even considered training herself, had she not quickly been put off by the atrocious politics at the Tavistock in the few lectures she had attended, she had added with a wry smile. That smile was an instant like for me – wit and spirit are rarely apparent in the same person within ten minutes. Anyway, as she grew up, she felt that she became more and more like her mother, warm and Irish and whole, and so perhaps therapy was not necessary after all.

It was in session four that Karen finally revealed her secret to me and I wish I could say that it didn't feel like a betrayal of all the warm feelings that I had allowed with eagerness to bubble between us, the ease with which I had accepted that it felt so pleasurable to sit in the room with her that it made me feel guilty for getting paid for it. How did she think I was supposed to receive 'the secret'? Just like another of our chats, deliciously comfy and fragrant like freshly ground coffee? That I would not get implicated, that I would only listen?

Freud warned therapists that they should be analysed enough not to have their own stuff intrude into the therapy. Thankfully, later psychoanalytic authors have been more forgiving. The truth is certain things never get soothed enough, no matter how much therapy one has. After my mother walked out on me/us when I was fourteen and my brother sixteen, all I could remember of her was that she had always been an abandoning and rejecting mother. Nothing else lingered. It didn't matter that we tickled each other in her big enveloping bed when I was little, it didn't matter that she took me out for coffee and shopping as soon as I reached my teens and for long holidays by the sea throughout our childhood; all that mattered was that she preferred to be elsewhere than with us, and that meant staying in an empty house with an increasingly work-preoccupied father when I needed somebody waiting there for me to come back from my explorations of the world. I don't know if I would have forgiven her if she had perhaps not had an affair. The blow only softened a tiny bit when I could finally make the connection between her departure and early death; yet to leave us for a life on an isolated island, apparently because life in the city was too hard for her, was just not on my palette of reasons for possible forgiveness. And now Karen, landing me with her secret, felt almost like an equal act of violation.

My eyes fell on the silver clock sitting comfortably at the centre of the coffee table, and I jumped. It was 9.57 am. Karen had never been late up to now, so for all I knew she was probably already in the waiting room. I was hoping to get rid of the coffee cup before she arrived. Without having fully realised it before, it occurred to me that neutrality of smell was an important focus of my practice. Why impose my morning habits on a patient? I opened the window wide and looked around the room. Where could I dispose of the cup of half-finished coffee? I settled for leaving it out of sight on a shelf by the small corner desk, the point in the room furthest away from the patient's chair. Another secret . . .

Karen was sitting comfortably in one of the brown leather chairs in the waiting area, the floor lamp next to her soothingly switched on to disperse the thick cloud and darkness outside the window. She wore her straight mahogany-coloured hair in a bob, and her reading glasses threw a warm colour on her hazel eyes as she was sitting cross-legged, holding a magazine without really reading it. She smiled when she saw me waiting by the door, and for an instant I was reminded of how fond I had been of her in the first few sessions, but the next feeling buzzed quickly in straight after, that I could not and would not forgive her.

'Come on in', I said, smiling too and holding the door open for her. I could not help but notice that she looked pale. I knew that look all too well, the look of insomnia, dark circles under and pink purple hues around the eyes. How come I knew her face so well already, as though we'd lived in the same house for a decade?

I could not resist asking her how she was feeling, an opening I found banal and impoverished to say the least, but one that, in this case, was indicating that, perhaps, I was aware that she was not feeling all that well.

'Well, I didn't sleep much last night', she said, and her voice sounded as tired as her eyes looked. 'I don't know if it was that I was coming here and my anxiety about what you made of what I told you last week or all the thoughts that kept flooding my head anyway or both.'

'What do you think I would have made of what you told me last week?' I asked trying to keep my voice very gentle.

'I don't know. I was hoping that you would tell me that.'

Five minutes into the session and there was tension already and that with somebody who was as smooth to be with as a gripping, well-written novel read under the breezy shade of a beach umbrella.

'I could, but I think that it may be important to explore what feelings you imagine I would be left with after your disclosure.'

'OK . . .', she cleared her throat. 'Well, there is a reason I didn't tell Tim, I mean there is a reason I haven't told anybody. I didn't quite expect to elicit sympathy. This is why I came here, I guess, hoping that perhaps a therapist can do this, have sympathy for my situation.'

I nodded and felt tears not far from creeping out. Tears of guilt or anger?

'But I wonder what it would mean for me to take your revelation in my stride, Karen. Would it not be like I don't care?'

'No, precisely the opposite, I think. It would be like you do care to listen to me and understand my perspective.'

Blood was pumping in my ears. This really did sound like my mother. *'See it from my perspective, Ellie.'*

'You have young children, Karen. How could I understand your perspective that you are choosing to die on them? I don't even know what the legal implications of my position are. Effectively, to just sit and listen to your perspective is like . . . is not far from harbouring a patient's suicide. It presents me with a huge ethical dilemma. Do you understand?'

Here, I said precisely what I thought, uttered all breathlessly in the space of two minutes. My feelings were plain to see now. I held my breath waiting for her response.

She leaned backwards fully supporting herself on the slightly reclining chair, eyes shut, hands holding on to the arm rests, as though she was suffering from vertigo.

'When I met Tim', she said, eyes still closed, 'I was drawn to him, I thought, because he was the exact opposite of my father. He was gregarious, fun, an adventurer. The only minus, he was a doctor of course, like all of us in my family. Doctors marry doctors for some reason. Anyway, after twenty-plus years of being with somebody, you just know them well enough to have a clear image of how they will respond to any given situation, and if you are lucky enough, this does not mean that they are boring or even worse, that you are bored. This is the case with us. I just know that no matter how open-minded Tim is, he would just not understand my choice. I hoped that the right therapist may help, and when I came to see you I felt so lucky, first time round of seeing a therapist and bang! You were clearly the right one, I felt such affinity with you from the first five minutes. And now this. I am so disappointed . . .'

'I am sorry that you are disappointed', I muttered.

In the silence that followed we both stared at the floor. It was the first time I was noticing the opulent shades of red and blue woven together in the carpet fabric. If only I could stop myself from being so full of tears, perhaps I could still help her.

'Karen,' I said leaning forward, trying to establish eye contact, I already missed the natural flow between us, as though she was already gone, 'would you go through with me again the specifics of your diagnosis? It was a lot to take in at the end of the last session.'

She smiled at me, as though I was about to have a consultation with her, an anxious patient presenting her with lots of questions. *She must be so deliciously maternal with her patients. A knot in the stomach.*

'Look, it is simple. You may have even heard it in the news or read about it. One in eight women is currently diagnosed in the UK with breast cancer. There are two possibilities, either we are facing an epidemic of unprecedented magnitude or we are dealing with overdiagnosis. The question is, are we facing an evolutionary problem where eventually most women will have to battle a deadly disease and have the most feminine part of their bodies removed? This is not unlikely. It has certainly been recorded in animal species. Tasmanian devils, for example, are in danger of elimination, as virtually all of them have started developing brain tumours. But it is not an expected outcome for animals or humans. Cancer is not a natural development. It points to adverse environmental factors like heart disease does. Of course, there is also a more logical possibility when it comes to breast cancer in the West. Yes, women have a diet that upsets female hormonal balance, heavy on alcohol and the use of cosmetics plus pollution and so on, but ultimately the interesting fact is that no more deaths have been recorded from breast cancer since the fifties, even though at least five times more women are getting diagnosed every day. I am afraid this is not due to the advancement of the treatment methods. Chemotherapy in particular is as haphazard and dangerous as it used to be. Of course, many doctors would argue that it is due to the early diagnosis of the disease that the death rate has reduced, but there is another distinct possibility, that not all of these early diagnoses of supposed cancer would lead to advanced disease and death. Come on, we may lead an unhealthy lifestyle in the West, but why don't we see the same increase in other diseases, even more evidently affected by the environment, such as, say, heart disease?'

I was listening intently. She must be an excellent doctor, helping her patients think for themselves. Not readily willing to yield to the medical establishment. How unusual.

'Karen, what you just told me is fascinating. But can we focus on you and your diagnosis. I suspect, this is what your husband would argue back. Perhaps, he would say, let's look at the specifics of your situation. Perhaps this is the conversation you are avoiding?'

'You are on to something, I think.'

She smiled wryly and I let out a discreet sigh of relief that our rapport seemed to have been re-established.

'Well, my formal diagnosis is invasive ductal carcinoma. It sounds scary, I know.'

'It does', I hastened to add, feeling close to losing my patience. I disliked like nothing else being fooled and I could not help but think that she was taking the mickey out of me. Suicidality disguised thinly with medical jargon. *I'm not buying it.*

She looked at me intently, examining my face carefully. I tried hard to keep my facial muscles on neutral.

'The bottom line is the following though. This is a very small tumour, less than 1cm big, much smaller than that and even more crucially, it is not an aggressive tumour. But most crucially of all, I do not believe in these early diagnoses. And that is the one thing I cannot quite forgive myself for: going through with the biopsy.'

'Hmm.'

'Look, I was the one that took myself for the mammogram. I thought I detected something, but a week later it was not there. It was not palpable what I had, I was told, yet something was there indeed, apparently. Had I waited for another week, had I not consented to the biopsy there and then, had I said no then, it could well be that the supposed tumour would no longer be there.'

'Hmm.'

She paused. 'Do you believe me?' she said in a voice that sounded almost desperate.

'Would it matter if I didn't?'

'I suppose, yes. If not, I would not be here trying to explain all this to you, would I?'

'Hmm . . . I wonder if in a way you are practising for what it would feel like to tell the people in your life? You fear that if I don't believe you, other people in your life won't either? That Tim will turn out to be just like your father, cold and rational and dismissive of your feelings?'

She hesitated. 'Maybe, but the thing is, I am not planning to tell Tim. It is too much to ask somebody to carry the anxiety of my decision with me.'

She examined my face again, her gaze was soft, like melted chocolate. 'I think I have made my decision and I need to take responsibility alone for going ahead with it. I am not going to accept treatment. If you think knowing this is too much for you to carry as well, and it sounds like you are saying it is, today could be our last session.'

How can one feel stabbed with such softness? *Mum gave me a hug warm like a richly cushioned, silk-covered canopy bed, before she set off for the island. She had said I could visit her any time outside exams, she would come and pick me up from Athens airport. By the end of the summer, she was dead. I had only visited once reluctantly, furious at her departure, and I had no clue she was ill at all. How deceitful was that?!*

'But Karen, I am trying to grasp why you feel you have to take such an extreme decision', I muttered in a shaky voice. 'As I understand, you have a form of cancer perfectly treatable and with an excellent prognosis, and yet, you are choosing not to have treatment. How do you think your family will feel if a few years down the line you die of advanced cancer because of something that would have been perfectly treatable now? On top, they will then find out that you chose not to tell them about it?'

I was surprised by her tears, her chest moving up and down quietly, the flow constant like the release of heavy rain after a period of drought. I offered tissues which she declined. It occurred to me then, how much she was trying to contain things for me, to make it bearable for me. An unfair role reversal. *Was Mum doing the same? My poor Mum trying to save me from her pain? Not wanting to admit to herself that there is no pain felt by the mother that the daughter will not experience?*

I let Karen cry quietly for what felt like a long time. She told me about her two sons, sitting their GCSEs and A levels and how much she didn't want to upset them before they left home to explore the world. She told me how full of zest her own mother had been and how she taught her that taking a risk at the right time was all that mattered in life, being able to stand up for oneself and make a choice.

Just about ten minutes before the end of the session and while the torrential rain of her tears continued to fall steadily, I leaned forward and I softly took her left hand in mine. She did not flinch, not even a bit. By the end of the session, I knew it was pretty clear to both of us that we were going to take this journey together.

1 + 1 = 0

> Several themes run through this short story about the limits of the therapeutic relationship, the failure of the maternal, and the unspoken and hidden nature of sexual abuse. Here, we meet Natalie from 'On the beach', as a young woman in therapy. Having been sexually abused does not feature as one of the main underlying issues of the predicament she brings to therapy. I think it is not uncommon for abuse to remain unspoken, even in therapy, or even to be dismissed and minimised by the therapist. Inherently connected with such a dismissal is a sense of self as flawed and bad or disgusting. Such a sense of one's badness is enacted here in the context of the therapy relationship, and it only begins to become disentangled when the experience of sexual abuse is acknowledged and grappled with.

I never fully understood what Natalie meant when she said that having two mothers was like having none until the day she told me about her memory of that last day of summer on the beach when she was eleven. As far as I was concerned, having two mothers was far better than having none and every time she recounted her Greek summers by the sea, I got that sinking feeling in the centre of my chest – Mum leaving us, leaving me to spend her time on her favourite island of her childhood, before leaving life for good.

I have to admit that I was always sceptical about working with Greek patients, because of my complicated relationship with Greece, and what it meant for me. And if Natalie had been my first Greek patient, I would have given up any attempt to set up a bilingual practice. But by the time she walked into my consulting room two years ago, I had worked with a number of patients in Greek and I had just about started finding my words, how to say things to them that had always appeared fluent and easy to reach when speaking in English.

Coming to think of it, the theme of two was everywhere in my work with Natalie. Though she came to me because of my Greek surname, she hesitated in that first session and then decided that she would much rather speak in English after all. She was in her late twenties, a PhD student in anthropology at UCL, for which, as evidence of further brilliance, she was receiving a prestigious scholarship. She was also in a settled, secure relationship with a young man her age, who was clearly devoted to her. I was not really surprised to hear that, as I saw Natalie as somebody who had it all, intelligence, looks and natural charm. Yet, what we were facing was a complicated therapy relationship; to put it simply, Natalie liked me more than I liked her.

It is not that her story hadn't moved me. It was my main criterion for taking somebody on, that I needed to be moved by them. Or that there was not much affinity between Natalie and me: a love for literature, an inquisitive and critical mind, a similar privileged middle-class upbringing in urban Greece. And though I was not old enough to be Natalie's mother, in my early forties, I was more than old enough to feel maternal towards her. Even more perplexing was the fact that she appeared by all accounts to have developed a positive, almost idealising transference towards me, and so it was rather bizarre that her feelings were not reciprocated, as it usually happens in such cases. Natalie would walk in puppy-faced, gently taking the room in, glancing at me sideways, as though she wanted to assess the state of my health, to make sure I was all right. Then, she would breathlessly recount the latest events of the week making fluent links between the past and the present and what had brought her here. She was, in many ways, an ideal patient.

Natalie and Thomas had just got married. She had a strong unconventional streak and would have resisted her father's nudges were it not for the predicament that had brought her to therapy. It could be summarised as three is always best or one and one needs one more. Natalie said this was not the situation right from the beginning of her relationship. She had gone through an intense falling in love phase, where it felt like there was nothing and nobody else in the world than Thomas. She placed the beginning of the intrusion at the time they needed to be separated. When they had started dating at the end of high school, Thomas had already accepted an offer to study at a university in London and Natalie has successfully passed her entry exams at the Philosophy School in Thessaloniki, where they both came from. So, right from the beginning of the relationship, separation was looming ahead. Though Natalie dealt with it very rationally, understanding that it was essential for the relationship's survival that they both pursued their courses of study – in fact the in-love feelings were intensified for both of them through the miles they had to put between them – it was not long after Thomas's departure that she started experiencing what I would call the beginnings of a double life. It started with spending increasing amounts of time with a young man from her university year, who, like her, had identified anthropology as a specialised area he wanted to focus on. Natalie stressed to me how sought-after this young man was. He was handsome and intelligent and came from a fascinating and well-known family of academics and musicians. And even more importantly, unlike Thomas, he was available and keen to be with her, every day. Yet, her feelings for Thomas were even further intensified through the dilemma and so, even though she continued her frequent meetings with her university peer, she never seriously thought of taking it any further. This, Natalie said, set up a feeling of constantly living life on edge, as she was well aware that it was a very fine balance between the courtship she was, in fact, allowing to take place, and things getting to the next stage. She was also, she said, slightly guilty about looking like she was leading the young man on, and of course towards Thomas as well for what was an inevitable betrayal. The next stage of the situation was in fact Thomas becoming aware of the other man's existence through Natalie's self-disclosure, which in turn set up a triangular situation where every time Natalie was not happy with Thomas, which was increasingly often, she would point out that she was not considering other opportunities because of her commitment to him.

What had brought her to therapy was the quick onset of yet another of these situations shortly after they got married. In fact, the closest she had got to leaving Thomas was just before they got married, in a complicated situation involving another couple. The man was fragile and desperate for Natalie's attention and his courtship more persistent, daring and brave than she had experienced before. Things were perilous and she knew as much. Thomas's reaction was different as well. He was intensely jealous of the other man, who had previously been a close friend of his, and they had started rowing about him increasingly. The falling-out was hard and heartbreaking. Just before their wedding, the man and his girlfriend moved out of their flat which was just above Natalie and Thomas's studio and severed all contact with them abruptly. Yet, no longer than a couple of months after their wedding, the triangle was repeated again. This time, it took the form of a friend of a friend, newly settled in London, who was desperate for company. Soon enough, the three of them would hang out together most of the time, and though Thomas seemed unaware of the developing situation, Natalie could not help but be painfully conscious of the repetitive scenario.

***

'Here is the thing', I said with a sigh of frustration that breezy October morning six months after the beginning of our therapy work, when I finally decided to take Natalie to supervision. 'I know she has a complicated history, and objectively a painful one, but the girl is a brat. Sorry, I am expressing myself freely here, so that you can see my predicament, how I get flooded by all these negative feelings about her that I don't know what to do with.'

'Go on', Peter mumbled, sitting in his usual contemplative pose. It was a relief that, after three years of coming here, I could speak and act like myself, which was the only way really in which I could find supervision helpful.

'Well, she is a spoiled brat, isn't she? She has a committed boyfriend who is in love with her, and on top of that she is in love with him, and then, she involves all these other men, leads them on and then breaks their heart. How much sympathy can one feel for her?'

'The point is, Ellie, that you don't feel for her, even though you are aware of her pain and this is where you are stuck.'

'Quite!'

'Can you tell me a bit more about her complicated history?'

'She has had two mothers.'

'Two mothers?'

'Yes. Her father was a philanderer. He and his wife could not have children which made his infidelities even more frequent and persistent. He got one of his long-term girlfriends pregnant and came up with the plan to encourage her to have the baby and to give her away for adoption to his wife and him. This baby girl is Natalie.'

'This is a complicated history!'

'It gets even more complicated than that. He never really separated from his girlfriend. He managed to persuade his wife to have her involved in Natalie's upbringing as a kind of nanny. For the first six years of her life, Natalie saw her birth mother on a daily basis, but she didn't know who she was.'

'And then?'

'Then the whole triangle fell apart, not sure why. The birth mother moved away to another city for a while, but this did not last either. Eventually she returned and they continued with their affair, but she was no longer allowed into the house. She was the father's secret girlfriend that everyone knew about.'

'And how did Natalie experience her birth mother's departure?'

'She was not fully conscious of what was going on, but what she does remember very clearly is that the first five years of her life she had a number of nannies and the father's girlfriends were parading around the house. These years she says, surprisingly, were very happy, but everything changed afterwards. She remembers being in the house with her two parents only as a kind of prison.'

'Hmm! She must have been picking up on her parents' unhappiness and sense of entrapment in their marriage.'

'I guess!'

'But, I am wondering about your feelings', Peter said, rubbing gently his beard, a gesture I had by now come to understand as contemplative and, perhaps, a little puzzled as well. I liked seeing Peter. He was the third in a series of male supervisors I had seen in the last six years, since I reached enough seniority in my practice to not have to see one at all.

Sometimes, I wished my relationship with men in real life was as easy as with these supervisors. It was my choice to see them. None of them was a perfect fit, yet I liked working with each one of them in different ways, and at some point, at least with the two before Peter, we had reached the limits of our work together and it was easy then to say goodbye. This was the bit I liked the most about working with them and which I had never found easy in my private life; Accepting somebody's imperfections, building a good relationship with them, and then letting them go when the time is right without feeling betrayed and heart broken. The trouble was, falling in love always messed things up. Maybe, this was exactly the thing with Natalie as well, falling in love made her feel at risk.

'So, your feelings sound to me like you are leading Natalie on', Peter went on. 'I mean, on the surface, it looks like you like her and have a smooth relationship, while underneath that, you are, let's face it, quite envious of her, and she seems to be rather oblivious to this.'

The word 'envious' stung me like a wasp. I opened my mouth to protest, but then closed it again. This was one of the things I liked about Peter, he named things quickly and accurately, even if what he said was sometimes hard to digest.

'So, my question to you is, do you think Natalie may have also been led on somehow? By one of her mothers perhaps or by the whole set-up in her mad family?'

***

I had almost completely forgotten that conversation with Peter until about a year and a half later, when on another breezy April day, Natalie walked in, somewhat more solemn and less eager to please than her usual demeanour. She sat in the green velvet chair opposite me rather heavily and stayed silent for quite a while.

Since that supervision session with Peter, I had admitted to myself rather reluctantly that envy was what I felt; a shameful feeling to have towards a patient, especially as she happened to be a young woman in distress. But, let's face it, I was probably not the first therapist to experience envy towards her young bright female patient. Yet, to be envious of one's patient seemed to me like the ultimate failure of maternal containment. I could not help but compare myself with her unfavourably and find me lacking. Paradoxically, since admitting to myself my failure to be the therapist Natalie needed, a certain tenderness had managed to creep into my repertoire of feelings towards her. So, that April morning, I managed to feel a degree of concern and sadness about her dark state of mind. Eventually, after five minutes of silence, which in the subjective rolling of time that made up a session felt like centuries, I asked her what was up.

'I am just in a low mood, not sure why', Natalie shrugged her shoulders.

As I often do in these cases, when things feel stuck in a way that's obstructing the appearance of the monster hiding round the dark corner, I took a leap of faith and fed back to her the irrational rumblings on my mind. It felt like disappointment, I said, as though Natalie was for whatever reason disillusioned. Disillusioned with somebody, even with me? And then, her tears starting flowing at last. She had been apparently sitting on this dream she had shortly after our last session a week ago, forgetting it, but then the images would creep back in, and since then, her mood had been heavy.

It was not the first time that I had seen Natalie in a depressive state. In fact, this was an obvious point of connection between us. Her moods would fluctuate from being on top of things, the world being her oyster, to this deeply unloved pessimistic and deadly state. I had seen her go through the cycle before, and yet, I was right to sense that this time something was different.

'Would you like to tell me about your dream?' I said gently.

'I was on a boat with my parents. It was OK and smooth to start with, a beautiful summer day, and then, it came to a halt. As I looked down, I saw that water had come in and the boat was sinking. There were other people and they were all panicking and my father said, we need to get out and swim. He was looking at me and not my mother, so I thought he meant the two of us had to be saved.'

I held my breath, intuitively knowing that we were in new, darker territory, and yet, despite my undivided attention, I noticed the feeling taking over again, resentment, bitterness that even in her dreams, Natalie was the chosen one, the golden girl.

'Then, we were in the water, but as we were swimming, he started touching me and kissing me and he was so forceful that I started drowning and he was still all over me.' She burst into tears.

'Do you mean your father was touching you sexually?' I mumbled in sudden shock.

'Yes . . . but the worst is to come. Then, my mother was next to him and she took him by the arm completely ignoring me, and the two of them were swimming towards the shore. The sea was calm and glimmering and I was there in deep water, not quite drowning, but knowing I would not make it out either.'

After that, Natalie cried quietly for a long while, and I felt it clearly that she did not want me to intervene. When I finally spoke, we were past the middle of the session.

'What struck me the most in your dream', I said finally, 'is how hateful your mother's role is. She takes your father away from you, who, by the way, is not nice to you either, but she calmly abandons you to drown in the deep.'

'It's a screen memory. As I was telling the dream, as I was telling it to you, I realised it was a screen memory.'

'A screen memory?'

'Yes, isn't that what Freud called them? When a dream brings up a forgotten childhood memory? Well, not that forgotten either to be honest.'

I sank in my chair quietly wanting to disappear. I was feeling more and more confused.

'I mean, not all of it happened like in the dream, but I get it. Now I told you the dream, I just get what it's about.'

I have heard that often as a half-joking complaint from friends and colleagues, *why is it we are doing this job?*, and though I have always gone along with this whingeing, I never really shared the sentiment, as in truth, I just love my job. Yet, at times like this, when I was just about to discover a particularly dark path in the already turbulent field of a patient's life and I was also made to feel incompetent for not having a sense of it before, I had to wonder if it was the right profession for me indeed.

'Are you trying to tell me that your father sexually abused you?'

'No, not my father really.'

'But?'

'A cousin.'

'A cousin?'

'Yes, that incident in the sea happened for real, but not with my father. He was forcing himself on me and I was nearly drowning. It went on for many years but that was the one time my mother found out about it.'

'Natalie,' I said stressing my every word, 'you have been sexually abused for many years, and you've been coming here for two and never told me?'

'It sounds like you are scolding me', Natalie half-smiled her girly smile and I sensed that she was trying to please me again. 'Well, he was just an older cousin, quite a bit older to be honest. It was more like bullying me and I detested him. He was disgusting!'

'So, you didn't think I would make much of it?'

'I guess!'

'Like your mother didn't on that day on the beach?'

'How do you even know?' she looked at me with big, staring eyes, her beautifully innocent eyes I had failed to bond with up to that day.

We spent the rest of that session recovering Natalie's memory of that day on the beach. How her mother had remained apparently oblivious to her cousin's harassment. How he had got over-excited about having Natalie all to himself in the sea. How he took more and more sexual risks with her until an old lady, horrified by the scene, went to alert her mother. That was the moment of rescuing that Natalie was hoping for for years now. Her mother would tell her cousin off, would alert her father and the horrible thing would never take place again after that. But the moment never came. Natalie's mother continued ignoring the abuse, if anything letting Natalie know that it was all her fault. 'You are just like your father', she had said to her contemptuously.

Of course, the incident on the boat had also happened as well. It was a case of condensation, as Freud would have called it, two key incidents from Natalie's adolescence condensed in one. After much thought and putting the pieces together, Natalie was fairly certain that the incident on the boat happened during the same summer break, just a month or so earlier. They had taken a short boat trip with her parents during a week's holiday in the Peloponnese. The boat's engine had stopped in the middle of the trip, and water had started creeping in. Her father was alarmed and she remembered him telling her clearly that she and he could swim out if they needed to, and they would make it to the shore, but it would have to be the two of them as he would help her out. She also remembered her mother's face, expressionless while her husband was counting her amongst the casualties, but with a distinct glimmer of anger. In the thorough unpacking we did in the sessions to come, it was clear that during that late afternoon of a late summer day on the beach, her mother had chosen to prioritise her relationship with her own husband, who she could have all to herself when Natalie was sent off year after year to spend the long school summer breaks with her paternal aunt and the cousin in question, over Natalie's well-being.

We also discovered that, in the painful repetition with Thomas, not only did having two men on her mind feel like having two mothers and yet none, but also that the existence of a suitor who threatened her relationship with Thomas acted as a reminder of the intrusion of the abuse. By letting Thomas know that another man was flirting with her, she was doing two things. She was endangering her relationship with him in a way that could prove catastrophic at any point, but she was also asking for his help and alertness in keeping the intruder out. She was in other words constantly walking on the cutting edge of a sharp razor, suspended between keeping her balance, or being deeply wounded.

The moment she came to therapy, was the moment she had stopped believing that the balance could be kept, as she had convinced herself that she was bad to be leading all these men on and she deserved to be punished. It was this unbearable badness that had been deposited on me, both her hatred for herself, but also my own conviction that I was rather despicable to be having all these envious feelings towards her. So in all this mess, it was hard to see that neither of us was being led on, but that we both suffered from exactly the same wound, the failure of the maternal.

Thankfully, we never needed to discuss directly what Peter had called my complicated countertransference. There was not much of that left, as I grew warmer and more protective towards her. One thing I was right about though was the feeling I had picked up in the silence preceding the storm; Disillusionment. And indeed, this was what Natalie had to face up to in the sessions to come. How her mother was, and indeed both of her mothers were, much more geared to be her father's wives than do the mothering work. And as such, I was retrospectively grateful to Peter that he took me up on my therapist task of harbouring the space for Natalie. It felt like the more I gave to her, the more I could gain for myself and so, gradually, we could both stay with what was.

Lost love and how to find it

> I think most therapists would agree that they learn about themselves through their patients at least as much as they help their patients learn about themselves. There is a sense of satisfaction and nourishment when a session has helped us think clearly about life and its predicaments. This is more likely to happen when an exploratory conversation is harboured as a legitimate way to use the therapy space and to facilitate the therapy process. In this short story, a question is asked about the importance of feeling a connection with another in a close relationship, and what to do when we establish deep connections with people we no longer have in our lives.

I have to admit that I always feel slightly on edge when I am about to see a male patient for the first time, especially if he happens to be significantly older than me. It does put me more at ease, if the patient in question, like Giovanni Strata in this case, has happened to find me directly through my website, and even more, if he indicates that, after having looked at my profile, he would like to work with me. The reasons for choosing me that patients have presented me with over the last ten years since I built my website are always surprising and unexpected. But never nearly as surprising or unexpected as the reason Giovanni presented me with in his first (and last) early evening session.

An Italian name and the age of fifty-two geared my imagination towards expecting a charming and well-dressed middle-aged man, perhaps struggling to shift an extended midlife crisis. I was not wrong on the looks count. Giovanni was dressed in an airy white shirt not tucked in his designer jeans and a black raincoat, which he took time to fold neatly before asking for my permission to place it on the bottom of my couch. His lightly tanned skin, calm and alert face and relaxed body posture as well as the firm handshake he gave me at the door exuded a confidence that made me wonder what was possibly bringing him to a therapist's consulting room.

He worked as a travel agent, he said, which managed to combine two of his biggest passions, travelling and reading.

'I did a lot of solo travelling when I was younger, but as I settled in my thirties with a wife and now three teenage boys, I travelled less and read more and more. Travel books and fiction set in all the places I hadn't yet been to. It is reading that has actually brought me here, but not travel reading. Alain de Botton.'

'Alain de Botton?' I muttered, feeling even more on edge.

'Yes, the romantic philosopher.'

'Hmm?'

'You and him have a lot in common as well as others in your profession.'

He paused and looked at me with an amused smile that wrinkled his eyes. It was a relief that fifty-two was considered nowadays a charming age for a man, and that women were catching up soon. I would be there in less than ten years and I had not even begun to settle on an answer to the question of whether to give up on my half-hearted wish to try and have a baby with Luke or not. This man seemed to have gone through the life stages and to have come through the other end relatively unscathed.

'You seem puzzled', he persisted.

'I am', I said smiling back. Most of the time, I preferred an honest answer to the supposed therapeutic neutrality that failed to deliver.

'Well, what I mean is that you, like a number of your colleagues I looked up, but you in particular, focus on the importance of relationship and how therapeutic it is.'

I nodded, intrigued to know where this was going.

'So?' I said after a while when no more clarification was forthcoming.

'So, I think you are wrong and I wanted to meet a professional in person to talk it through. I was prepared to pay a full fee just so that I can argue my case. I have been thinking about it a lot, you see.'

I tried hard not to feel defensive, but whenever I had heard somebody before trying to convince me that they were visiting a therapist for academic reasons and not through the urgency of their suffering, even if unwittingly, it had got my back up. I should have known better than jumping to the next conclusion or interpretation, but I could not resist leaning forward and asking him:

'Is the problem that you are in an unhappy relationship?'

After all, the clock was ticking and, as he had mentioned already, he was going to pay my full fee.

'Not at all. As I said already, I am not coming here to solve a problem in my personal life, but one that has preoccupied my mind in the last few months, and that if I don't manage to find some peace with soon, it might well become a personal problem.'

'Was there something that triggered the problem? You mentioned it occurred in the last few months.'

'Look, unlike what you suggested, I am very happily married. I met my now wife in my thirties and she is also from Italy, although a different part than where I come from. I come from the South and growing up there marks you for ever. It is such a culturally binding place. This is the best way I can possibly describe it.'

'Hmm.' I knew all about culturally binding places from my mother. How she spent all her life trying to avoid being defined like that, how ironically she was desperate to die in the very same place she ran away from for all her adult life, almost falling back into all the rituals she taught us to look down on.

'I come from Messina in Sicily. A small place, growing up near the sea, not much money and you know, all the rumours about the Mafia are true. The Mafia is one of the ways in which the place defines your life. I mean either your family are in it or not, and if they are not, and my family were not, thank God for that, you spend your life trying to avoid it. Anyway, it is so many years now since I moved away and what has stayed with me, what I am still carrying is the landscape and the sea, you know.'

He tousled his hair and I thought I could almost see in his wrinkled skin and the discreet lemony scent that came through, the salt-sculpted rocks, the seagulls and the wind-bent pines of his homeland, not that far from the place of birth of my mother.

'You are very right indeed, it was an incident during a short visit back home that has started these thoughts and my mind will not rest since. But before I get there, can I tell you what I meant about Alain de Botton?'

I nodded noticing I had not, even slightly, shifted in my seat, I had not even uncrossed my legs, my right leg getting numb now under the weight of the other, so intent I was to hear what he had to say.

'In his early work, Alain de Botton describes what it is like to fall in, and also to fall out, of love. Well, this is not quite the same with staying in love, being in a loving relationship, is it?'

'I guess it is not', I muttered.

'The thing with you therapists, though, and honestly, I spent the last three months looking at therapists' websites before picking you, is that you romanticise relationships, you say they are therapeutic, it is what we all want and need, but not the emptiness of companionship or the convenience of marriage, the thrill of a connection that lasts. Somebody who connects with our soul. Right?'

'Well, that seems to make many assumptions at once, but I would agree that a connection, a genuine one, is part of a good enough relationship.'

'But if you look at falling in and out of love, it is something random that attracts us to somebody, and this something seems like the most important thing in the world, but once it is gone, that's it, it doesn't matter at all, and the person no longer matters either.'

I uncrossed my legs before I lost all feeling in them, and the thought crossed my mind that legs didn't matter as all. My energy was now focused on my head and my gut.

'Look,' I said, 'I think you are confusing two things, a crush, what most young people have at some point, and more mature relationships, when things begin to go wrong, and the true intimacy built in a long-term relationship that can lead to a long-lasting connection, if one works on it.'

'All clichés, I am afraid, same like in all the websites of your colleagues and yours', he added.

'Really?' I nearly snapped as I felt the blow of his insult tighten my throat. 'And why did you pick my website then, may I ask?'

'Because unlike other therapists, you do not just mention relationships as the epitome of normality, but the connection too. Look, I've got it memorised, you say, 'it is the unique connection between two people in the context of the therapeutic relationship that can invariably prove healing.'

'And so?'

'So, the two are not the same thing. I mean by that that if you are a cynic you believe that a relationship is an arrangement of some sort between two benefiting partners. If you are a romantic though, and permit me to say that most of you therapists are, you believe that you are in a relationship because of the unique and, to a degree, special connection you have with a particular person and that the number of people you can have such a connection and relationship with is limited. So if you believe that, then the question is how can you ever fall out of love or even worse, forget somebody you once loved? This is exactly the question I came to ask your opinion about.'

'Do you mean then that it is somewhat disingenuous to claim a connection with somebody is important, if this connection can be easily lost or forgotten?'

'Yes, precisely that.'

I looked at the clock, anxiety starting to take over. He was right of course, and the problem was I had no idea how to answer his question. I thought of her again, the deepest connection ever, that with one's own mother, being carried inside her, fed from her body, her body a cushion for one's growing being, my mother's eyes and voice and the way she giggled through her nose, which was so utterly contagious, especially when she was near her summerhouse by the sea on a sunny day, all this was so not forgotten. I could see her throwing her head back and laughing under the sun as though it was only yesterday, yet it was over twenty-five years since her death. Twenty to six, only ten minutes to go. He came after all with a valid question to ask a therapist and I had no answer to give him at all.

'It was a late September evening at the end of last summer in my hometown. A work visit, part of my research for my travel blog. I tailor-make holidays for the discerning traveller, you see, and I strongly believe that late September is the absolutely best time to visit Sicily. The summer nearly dying, the light in the evening growing melancholic, yet the air full with the scent of sweet ripe summer fruits. I was walking past my old neighbourhood when she stopped me and, in the unique way of women from the South, she gave me a tight hug that felt so heart-warming. The trouble was I had no idea who she was. So I was standing there, chatting warmly with her, answering questions about my family and as this woman clearly knew me so well, there was no way I could have said, 'Excuse me, can you remind me who you are?'. Has that ever happened to you? It is so embarrassing, so awkward. And you are always left wondering if that person has sussed you out and she knows you are pretending and you have no idea who she is. Cleo was her name. She came to my dream the night after I met her. Her delicate smile, the dimples on her cheeks, even the other more intimate dimple on her lower back came to my dream. She was the first girl I ever fell in love with. And I had no idea who she was, can you believe that? I bumped into her in the very same neighbourhood where we used to meet for our late evening dates, thirty years later, and she had not even changed that much. Still as elegant and beautiful, and yet, a complete stranger.'

'This must have been disconcerting, and I can see that you found it strange that you could not remember who she was.'

'The thing is it is not that strange in fact. It was only a short summer fling. But the intensity of it, and the fact that she was so different from all the other girls I had ever met. I have had a teenage sweetheart before and other short flings as well, but she was just not like any of the other girls at all. She wanted to go all the way from the beginning, you know, and you could feel it was like . . . this is what she felt like, her body was fully in it, not self-destructive, not rebellious or lost or breaking a taboo, just fully present with me.'

'But then, panic set in. My older brother spotted us by the beach once and that was it, the word spread and my parents were so worried. There were rumours about her father and uncles, you see, that they were hard-core Mafiosi, dangerous people.'

'Ooh!'

'She is the girl that set me free, you know, it gave me the push I needed to leave home, to travel the world, to find myself.'

'Well, you seem to have just given the answer you came to me for, very clearly', I said leaning forward and glancing at the clock. Only three minutes to go and I had a patient at 6 pm who always arrived promptly. Had he also given me the answer to a question that had unwittingly bothered me too for all my life? I felt the release of tension throughout my body and the relief of having reached some resolution for a life-long conflict.

'Did I?' he said, looking puzzled.

'Yes, indeed! You see this girl was a catalyst. She taught you something about being true to yourself and present in your life. You took her with you in all your travels, she became you. I mean, she became a fully integrated part of you. Meeting her gave you permission to go places in life. So, you did not need to remember her, as there was nothing you still needed as such from her. She was all inside you.'

'That's a very interesting take, I guess', he said seeming deeply buried in thought.

As I was accompanying him to the door, I thought of all the brief encounters and some longer ones I had with patients in my first years of practice. It occurred to me that I could hardly remember their faces or names or stories, yet they were all sitting alongside me in this room during this brief encounter with Giovanni.

I reciprocated his warm, firm handshake by the door.

Flat landscape

> One of the main underlying questions in this short story is what happens to our feelings when, for whatever reason, we find it really hard to own up to something. Of course, psychoanalysis, and more specifically Kleinian theory, has established a clinical term for this phenomenon, 'projective identification'. When certain feelings are unpalatable for the patient, the therapist may experience them as their own irrational thoughts and/or bodily reactions. In a more relational and intersubjective understanding of the therapy process, though, one could say that therapist and patient connect through their wounds, in this case, the disavowal of love and attachment towards a mother figure, who is experienced instead as persecutory. This short story is also about the importance of our early affectionate bonds, the loss of which is invariably difficult to mourn without allowing oneself to be open to one's helplessness.

When I set off for my consulting room on Monday morning, if would have been impossible to know if it was late evening or the middle of the night or any other pitch-dark hour. The roads had not been cleaned from the weekend indulgences, empty bottles lined up near doorsteps and the bins were piled high with leftovers of takeaway food. Thankfully, I was operating on a tight schedule and I knew exactly what time it was. 7.03 am on one of the darkest days of the year, shortly before Christmas.

This was going to be my last session with Claire before my holiday break. I was about to board the overground train that would take me to the east of London in fifteen minutes exactly, my consulting room being five minutes' walk from the station. If all went to plan, I would be the first to open the premises at 7.25 am, my session with Claire starting at 7.35 am, which would allow her in turn to be at her office which was round the corner at 8.30 am exactly.

When I stepped off the train, I noticed no change in the darkness all around me other than the Christmas lights, opulent in this part of London. Claire and I had been working together for just over a year now, and she had always arrived at 7.35 am on the dot, never a minute early or late. She was also always impeccably dressed – a feminine suit with a few touches, usually in the form of a flowery scarf. Her blonde hair was perfectly coiffed and her discreet make-up evenly applied. This made sense, of course, as Claire was the PA of a senior executive in a hedge fund and she just could not possibly hold such a position, she claimed, if she was not impeccable throughout. She did not nevertheless pretend to be happy or that she could possibly even know what being happy felt like, and just like the daylight never showing any intention of coming through during my brief journey to work today, I really could not see how I could help Claire feel any better.

The other problem we had was agreeing on the definition of what she was there for. She came for what she described as a flatness, a lack of joy in anything, as if she was operating her life through a remote control rather than living it. She was one of these people for whom even a detailed therapy assessment could easily reveal no more than dreary normality; she had a long-term boyfriend, they never argued, they had good routines of eating healthy meals together, occasionally going out with friends, travelling during their planned holidays, sex twice a week and both working long hours in ambitious, but established and risk-averse city jobs. Neither wanted children. The other thing Claire and her boyfriend, Mark, had in common was that they had very little contact with any family at all. They both had elderly parents living in the countryside, with whom they exchanged cards a few times a year. They had even given up the obligatory Christmas visit with the good enough excuse of finding it easier to travel abroad during the Christmas break, because of pressure at work, finding little resistance to the idea on either side of the family.

But there was one thing that was not that normative in Claire's history and which had nearly escaped my detailed initial assessment. She was adopted. Looking at her coloured white-blonde hair, perfectly suiting the translucent tone of her fair skin and her sky-blue eyes, it was still hard to remember that Claire's biological origins were Argentinian rather than consistent with the English upper-middle-class family she had been brought up in. Her birth mother was a maid in Claire's adoptive family and when, through an unusual incident, she revealed to Claire's adoptive mother the pregnancy and her plan to have an abortion, Claire's mother, Lucille, as Claire preferred to call her nowadays, persuaded the maid to keep the baby and to hand her over to Lucille, who would adopt her after birth. Lucille's plan was actually grander than that. She liked Sofia, Claire's birth mother, for a number of reasons. She was a young woman of exceptional and aristocratic beauty. She was also polite, prompt and effective in her work. On the other hand, Sofia had a warm, sunny side. Lucille had overheard her talking to her friends on the phone when she had finished her shift, and though her Spanish was not fluent, she had picked up the closeness in the tone of voice, the warmth missing like the sun from their family home.

Lucille longed for a girl, having had three boys in quick succession, and though she could not guarantee that a girl was what was growing in Sofia's discreetly expanding stomach below her still elegant, small waist, she was willing to take the risk. The day she walked into the kitchen and found Sofia silently weeping and looking out onto the rolling hills outside the large kitchen window, and soon after Sofia confided in her that she had missed three periods and that a pregnancy test had confirmed what she dreaded, the plan was in place in Lucille's mind.

It was unusual for Lucille to be in the kitchen at all. Her household was one where maids loved to work, as they were given good accommodation, they were not asked to work overtime and they had much freedom to run things in the way they deemed appropriate. Lucille was a landscape painter, and she spent most of the day in the loft painting the same landscape again and again, trying to capture the change of light and the seasons. She had noticed Sofia because of her exceptional looks, and her impeccable manners, but other than that, her wish was to be left alone to paint, and the more freedom and generosity she granted her maids, the more likely it was that this would happen. On the February morning when she walked into the kitchen, it was to give more instructions for a special occasion. She was hosting a special dinner party for her fortieth birthday, and as part of it, she was going to display a number of her landscape paintings.

Lucille would not think of or even describe herself as maternal, Claire had stressed to me. At forty, she was hugely relieved that her declining fertility, along with a firm message given to Richard through moving her bedroom up to the loft, meant no more babies. Yet, the moment she found Sofia weeping in the kitchen, something deeply maternal was set in place or at least this is what she conveyed to Claire. She held Sofia in a tight hug for a long time, telling her how honoured she was she had confided in her, telling her it would all be all right now. She would be taken care of. She could have the baby safely under Lucille's excellent physician's supervision, and Lucille was happy to quietly adopt the baby, if Sofia did not want the stigma. At that moment, she told Claire, the plan was set in place.

She and Sofia would develop a close bond during her pregnancy. She would relieve her of all domestic duties on the condition that she would act as a life model for two to three hours a day for Lucille. The thought of fulfilling her dream of developing her portrait skills through painting Sofia's divine pregnant body seemed to Lucille like a godsend. She was already fantasising about it, knowing that the forthcoming change of seasons from winter to spring to a burning yellow summer would be the most exciting time of her life. Through all this, she would also develop a close bond with the growing foetus, which she was convinced at that moment was a girl. It would be like she was the mother of that girl already, knowing her habitat inside out. And then, after the baby girl was born, Sofia would take great care of her. She would breastfeed her of course, and bond with her and never need to be separated at all, as the three of them could continue the journey together all along.

'Grand plans never work', Claire had said to me, the sarcasm dark and treacly in her voice despite her flat tone. This was during session three of a protracted assessment, while I was waiting patiently, almost holding my breath, for any feeling to emerge in Claire, as an expected response to the high drama of her story. And indeed, things did not go according to plan, not at least in any way that Lucille could have predicted. She spent, as she had dreamed, numerous late afternoons and early mornings, Lucille's favourite times for capturing the right light for her paintings, painting Sofia's increasingly pregnant, but still delicate body. She had been timid about introducing the idea of a nude, but Sofia had got it straight away, asking her whether she needed her to remove her clothes with the professionalism, neutrality and commitment that she had always demonstrated in her work for the Jardine family. In fact, Claire confessed to me in session five that the closest she had ever got to 'losing it' was when she had visited unsuspecting the Portrait Gallery to see the exhibition of Kate Moss's nudes. She had never thought of it before, but something in Moss's expression, neutral, almost indifferent, unreadable, as well as her fair features, reminded her straight away of her birth mother.

'So, you have seen your mother's nude portraits?' I hastened to intercept, only to get a frosty look back.

'Yes, during that period of my life, the darkest, as far as I am concerned, Lucille had shown me my birth mother's portraits. The only thing is that she had forgotten to ask me if I wanted to see them, if I even wanted to know.'

Lucille's attachment to Sofia and to the growing baby grew along with the pregnancy. During the period of their long conversations, she admitted to Claire that she felt rather ambivalent about the impending birth, sad about losing her life model and the inevitable uncertainty about the product of the gestation. Her fears were quickly pacified though. The newborn, a girl indeed, as she had always known, was as beautiful as her mother, a good baby as well that slept and fed in an easily established routine. And as for her fears of losing her life model, those were wrong as well. Lucille had never breastfed any of her boys, thanking the advance of technology for the introduction of convincingly healthy formula that could be fed through a warm bottle in the hospitable lap of one of her live-in nannies. Yet, when Sofia started breastfeeding the newborn girl, as Lucille had indicated she was hoping she would do, the sight of mother and baby, the subtle smells and sounds, the visible changes in the face of both before and after, gave Lucille the most inspiration for painting she had ever had. The bliss was not meant to last though, as early on a foggy November morning, she was woken up from unheard before wails. Next to the baby's crib, on the dark-green velvet cover of the perfectly made single bed Sofia had installed next to the baby, she found her note stating that by the time Lucille read this, Sofia would already be boarding a plane to Buenos Aires, where she was planning to live for the rest of her adult life.

I could not help but let out a terrified 'Ooh!' when Claire told me this part of the story. It was early days then, but it did not take me long to realise that the more emotion I showed to Claire, the more apathetic she appeared to be. After composing myself, I added:

'But why? Do you understand why your birth mother left so abruptly?'

'She was being exploited, I guess.'

'Was she?'

'Well, she was being used by Lucille as her life model. She probably didn't even want to have the baby, I mean me. At what point was she asked what she wanted?'

One of the many issues of incongruence that Claire and I were facing was our different feelings towards Lucille. Of course I never shared my feelings towards

Lucille with Claire. I also did not fully understand why they were coming through so strongly. It was rather strange, but I just adored Claire's adoptive mother. She seemed to me like a woman that, despite being in many ways a slave of her class, had managed to maintain aliveness throughout her life under no easy circumstances. Claire, on the other hand, despised her adoptive mother. She portrayed her as a self-absorbed and self-serving woman who had never been a mother to her or to any of her other children. Though I understood why Claire felt this way, it almost seemed that all my empathy and connection that should have belonged to my relationship with Claire, had been transferred to her mother.

The fall-out after Sofia's departure was hard for all concerned by the sound of it. Lucille went into a panic and then a depression which meant withdrawing even more into her loft for most of the day, refusing even to attend the family meals, which had been the fabric of daily life before. Thankfully, it was not hard to find nannies to step in, but interestingly, Claire did not remember any of them in particular. Claire's fondest memories of her childhood were of her father from the age she started attending pre-school to the time of being sent to boarding school at seven like all children across generations of the Jardine family

It was her father who taught her life, Claire said to me. He expected her to sit round the table with him and have her regular three meals a day, he took her out on long countryside walks, he talked to her about wild animals, plants and the change of the seasons. Richard was a successful architect and had previously travelled a lot for work, but since Sofia's departure, Claire remembered her father's presence in the house like the glue that held everything together. He was also the only person who was able to drag Lucille out of her refuge, even if only to attend family meals once or twice a day.

As for her mother, Claire remembers little of her during her early childhood, but it was what happened later that I think triggered Claire's contempt and even hatred of Lucille, not that Claire would ever own up to such strong feelings. Lucille's withdrawal and distant behaviour lifted as Claire approached adolescence. It is possible that the closer Claire got to becoming a young woman, the more Lucille saw in her a blooming, young Sofia. This is when Claire was fed in regular doses little portions of her history. Apparently, Lucille and Sofia had kept in touch over the years with what started as a rather formal Christmas card Sofia sent to the family that first dark Christmas after her departure, reassuring everyone that she was safe and well and asking hesitantly after her baby daughter. Over the years, the initial exchange of cards had developed into extensive long correspondence between the two women, the content of which Lucille had been reticent to share with Sofia.

Correspondence was also how it started all coming out during Claire's adolescence. She would receive a note from Lucille once a week, initially brief and curt, but increasingly, Lucille's letters would read like extracts of stories, many to do with Sofia, but also stories to do with other members of the family, some who Claire had hardly met and whose moment of fame preceded Claire's birth. Gradually, more feeling would seep into Lucille's notes as well, telling Claire how she always felt as close to her as though she was her only daughter and even closer than she ever felt to her boys.

'And you, how would you respond to Lucille's notes, to her expression of feeling?' I asked Claire in one of our first sessions, after I had given up hope that strong feelings would indeed emerge in her any time soon.

'This is the thing: to start with, my notes were very curt as well, but I have to say, I found Lucille's notes amusing and I began to look forward to them, even to rely on them. And then, I started writing back, telling her funny stories about what happened at school and there was always so much to narrate. We became pen pals.'

'So you grew really close to your adoptive mother.'

'I don't know', Claire replied shrugging her shoulders. I was now almost expecting her dismissive response every time I tried to introduce her to the idea of feelings. But that time, I decided not to relent.

'You were close to her, Claire, by the sound of it. She had become at that moment a strong attachment figure for you and you relied on her weekly contact to have a sense of aliveness during your week.'

Claire had told me that the sense of flatness she came to therapy for had started at boarding school. A sense that feelings did not exist, and though this was fine and more than fine, actually desirable, it meant that Claire could not experience joy in anything, even in things she used to love such as a walk in the countryside discovering small foraging animals and new plants, breathing in the fresh, humid air. Nothing would register any more. Of course, through my insistence and, perhaps, slight intrusion, I also came to realise that Claire had replaced her reliance on Lucille's notes to keep her alive during boarding school with her weekly reliance on the sessions. Claire never missed or cancelled a session, was never a minute late and she asked about my breaks well in advance so that she could schedule her own holidays around them.

'OK', she exhaled as though defeated. 'I guess I had started feeling close to Lucille during that period, if you want me to use your language, but in any case, this changed pretty quickly.'

'What made it change?'

'The kind of person Lucille was. It was all about herself in truth, and this became apparent to me very soon.'

'What happened?'

'In one of the long summers, I was home for, Richard was more absent than usual. I remember it was the first time I thought that, perhaps, he was fulfilling a duty that he had allocated to himself when I was younger, and that he no longer felt he needed to try with me. I actually remember feeling very sad, when I came to realise this.'

'Do you still think this is true?'

'Yes, I am afraid it is. Richard and I are like complete strangers now. It is just that he doesn't even know that I am still fond of him, but he is an old man now anyway, and I no longer see them . . .'

'And Lucille?'

'Well, that summer Lucille made a great effort. I remember it was just before sixth form, one of the last summers of being officially a child. She spent tea times with me. telling me more and more stories, despite my hints that I needed to study. And then, one stormy afternoon, we were sitting together in the music room, watching the lightning, hearing the violent shuffle of the leaves on the fruit-bearing late summer mature trees, when she suddenly got up and, silently, she went upstairs. I was thrown, not sure what to make of it. Five minutes later, I heard her footsteps heavy down the stairs, as she was carrying one of the large folders architects use to keep their drawings in. Richard must have given her one as a present. She nodded to me silently, while pulling sheets out of the folder, laying them on the floor, autumnal, spring, summer colours spreading rapidly on the carpet. I was familiar with Lucille's paintings. Many were beautifully framed and hang in the long corridors of the house as well as decorating the formal reception.'

'And were these paintings you had not previously seen?'

'To start with, the colours looked so familiar that I was expecting to see some more of her landscape painting, but as my eyes started to focus, I could see that these paintings were different. "What are these?" I mumbled breathlessly.'

'Were they the nude paintings?'

'Yes', Claire answered. 'And more than that.'

'More?'

'Yes, the breastfeeding ones as well.'

'Oh!'

Claire's upset was palpable in the room. I glanced at the clock. We had five minutes left, quietly I made the calculation that it would not take her as long to be in floods of tears. I also wondered silently if it would be OK to extend the session by ten minutes. Would that make her late at work? Would I manage the intensity of what was coming up with no break between this session and the next? I decided to play it by ear.

'Did you not know about these paintings beforehand?'

'This is exactly the thing, I did not know! Nobody had told me before then.'

'And?'

'I have to say, the nudes were beautiful. I don't know if my birth mother was truly such a beautiful woman, but what Lucille captured in her paintings was ethereal, the light in the background, the translucent blue veins on her white, vulnerable breasts, her innocent half-open mouth, her eyes clear like a cloudless sky. But what was really disturbing was the breastfeeding paintings. Some were traditional, "Madonna and Child"-like, but as she pulled more out laying them on the floor, I was shocked.'

'What was it, Claire?' I asked my breath being now almost cut away.

She stayed silent for what seemed like a shockingly long time. 'They were close-ups. The baby sucking the nipple, the skin of the breast stretching, Sofia's rosy cheeks and a rash on her chest. They were pornographic.'

'Do you mean they were about physical pleasure?'

'Yes, they were about physical pleasure of some perverse sort. I swore silently when seeing them never to have children, that I would never ever breastfeed.'

I opened my mouth to suggest gently that maybe what was so disturbing in what Claire saw in these pictures was the love between her and her mother and the love of Lucille for both, that she could not bear to see that, as she had never got to know that beautiful mother who abandoned her shortly after. That the intensity of the love and the passion captured in these paintings were too much for her to bear, as she would then know what she had lost for the rest of her childhood, maybe for ever. Of course, I would not have said as much as that, but these were my thoughts. Before I had time to open my mouth, Claire had got up quietly, telling me it was now 8.25 am and our session was over.

Claire told me in the following session that after Lucille's disclosure of the paintings, she retreated into her room for the rest of that summer holiday, pretending that the amount of homework she needed to complete before resuming school did not allow her to spend any time outside her room other than for sitting down for meals. She even requested that she had some tea and toast brought to her room for breakfast as this was the best time to have a clear head for studying, Lucille reacted as though she was expecting Claire's withdrawal and she quickly reverted to their earlier format of exchanging a few words about the weather and the food during family meals. Claire also blamed her failure to succeed in embarking on a science degree to Lucille's intrusion. Studying business instead felt like a further exclusion from the family's impressive academic credentials. Yet, it gave her a firm plan for becoming financially independent quickly and severing her bonds with the Jardine family at astronomical speed.

The only thing I had not tried for helping Claire to connect with the feelings of loss and sadness that I thought her flat mood was concealing was asking her what brought her to therapy after all, if her life was so well settled and as she wanted it, as I considered this to be rather harsh. As I recounted the sessions we had, though, on my dark early morning to work to conduct our last session for this year, I wondered if I had managed to help Claire at all, and for how much longer we could continue our hide-and-seek from her feelings before it felt like I was colluding with the hiding.

I never liked the smell the waiting room let out first thing in the morning, but as I switched on the light and gently lifted the kitchenette's window to let a breath of fresh air in, I realised that it was now a familiar smell that I had come to anticipate as part of my weekly routine. By 7.35 am, I had plumped the cushions in my consulting room, placed my glass of water next to my chair and I anticipated eagerly, if not without a sinking feeling in my chest, the buzzing of the electronic doorbell. When by 7.38 am, the doorbell had not buzzed, the dread feeling in my chest had become a tightening similar to being woken up in the middle of the night by the phone ringing, knowing fully well that such ringing has to mean a loved one's illness or even death.

Eventually, the buzzer rang at 7.53 am, by which time I was preparing to ring Claire. When she came in, I knew straight away that everything was different. I don't know if it was the fact that she was not dressed for work – her casual jeans and beige sweater still looked beautiful on her – or the fact that purple shadows underlined her eyes and made them look more like a winter dusk sky. I guess this is one of the most magical things about long-term therapy that hardly anyone talks about, that patient and therapist get to know each other's faces and cues like a mother with a newborn child. So, I just knew when Claire walked in that something major was wrong.

'Sorry, I am so late', she mumbled. 'I have hardly slept the night. I am taking the day off work, but I needed to get here.'

'I can give you an extra ten minutes', I muttered.

Then, silently, Claire passed me the letter.

'What is this?' I asked.

'It is from Lucille, please read.'

My dearest Claire, it began.

'Claire, are you sure you want me to read this rather than you telling me about it first?' I interrupted my reading, feeling apprehension as though I was about to encounter a mortal danger.

'Please do read it. I really cannot talk about it', she replied.

And at that moment, after fourteen months in therapy where not a single tear had been shed, Claire starting weeping silently. Finally, the small, wounded child was there in the room with me and I calmly got up, resisting my urge to give her a hug. Instead, I picked up the chequered blanket from the couch and threw it round Claire's shuddering shoulders, before settling back in my chair with the letter in my hand. Lucille's perfectly joined and yet easy to read writing unfolded in front of my eyes.

> *I know we have not been in touch for a while and I have to say, I always miss your presence in the house around Christmas and summer time. I hope you know that this is always your home and you are welcome to come and stay any time you want.*
>
> *As my health has somewhat deteriorated in the last year, nothing to worry too much about though, I felt that I had to share with you some important details of your history that you should know about once I am gone. I know that my revelations about your history over the years have not always been welcome and I wish to apologise to you both about the past intrusions and also about what I am about to disclose, which I believe will upset you.*
>
> *You may already know that your birth mother, Sofia and I have been in touch over the years. You may also have a sense that Sofia and I have had a very close bond and that we were both very grateful to have been in each other's life. The sad news I have to break to you is that Sofia has now died. I received a card from a member of her family informing me of her death a month ago. Sadly, Sofia got a bad strain of pneumonia that developed complications that in the end proved fatal. The letter also informed me that Sofia had left a will according to which all her savings and belongings, which apparently are considerable, need to come into your possession. I have delayed contact with the solicitor in Buenos Aires overseeing the case, so that I could write to you first. I think you will have to go over there, my darling. I hope you don't mind me calling you that.*
>
> *You may now wonder how come you have never met Sofia, despite the fact that she and I have always kept in touch, and despite the fact that she was*

so committed to you that she never married or had other children and she worked for all her life, saving to give to you. This was also partly my question at the beginning, soon after Sofa's departure. I could not understand why she left so abruptly and I felt mortally wounded by her departure.

I was right to suppose that I had somehow offended Sofia. When she eventually started writing to me, she confessed that even though the months of being pregnant and posing as a life model for me were the best of her life, everything changed after the birth. She had not been asked, she wrote, about whether she wanted to breastfeed or to even have the baby or even more to pose with the baby while breastfeeding. You see, I truly think your birth mother was an amazing woman, but her one downfall, which affected all her life, was that she could not say 'no', when it was important that she did. That meant that I made many assumptions about what she may have wanted, and I should not have. I think I may have made the same mistake with you.

Sofia was in love with your biological father, Claire. They were courting, not even dating. They met regularly at a tango parlour her and her friends frequented once a week. On the night of your conception, he asked her out and she assumed that this would be a date. One thing led to another and he also made many assumptions about what she wanted that he should not have. This was Sofia's first sexual experience, Claire, and it was traumatic. She never saw the man again and she severed all her ties with her Argentinian friends in London after that. She was in touch with one friend only, who helped her organise her escape.

But there is an upside, Claire, there truly is. Sofia and I wrote to each other in a way that we did not write to anybody else. These letters are all saved in a folder for you to see, if you choose to. Even though her escape was her way of saying no, she felt that through me, she could have a daughter whose existence she cherished. She wanted you to know after her death how proud she has been of you and how closely she followed your development through my updates . . . .

I stopped reading and looked at Claire who had stopped weeping and was sitting quietly, curled up in the armchair like a little girl sipping a hot chocolate. I warmed to her. I knew all too well about family secrets and revelations and their lasting wounds.

'I get the picture', I said tenderly. 'It will be all right.'

Claire nodded and tears started rolling down her face again. She smiled at me, a smile of trust and affection. At that moment, I knew that we were at the beginning of a journey, where her attachment to me, and to Lucille, would no longer have to be repressed and flattened out.

Clinical polygamy

> This story is, to an extent, about a well-known phenomenon in clinical work, repetition compulsion, which Freud identified from early on. When a patient acknowledges from the beginning of therapy that they are caught up in repeating the same pattern, the hope is that the repetition will cease, while at the same time, what is also at play is setting up an expectation for both parties of the therapeutic dyad that the pattern will be repeated during the therapy process one way or another. Another theme here is around trust and betrayal. A question is being raised about whether the therapeutic relationship is based on the hope that both parties will do their best not to hurt one another.

As a therapist, I have often thought *I have been with this kind of person before, and this is the kind of thing that may crop up.* This was not the case with Cedros Droscsz. The morning he sat in the client's chair with no hesitation at all for his ninth session, for a split second I forgot that he was there as my most recent patient to embark on the journey of psychotherapy and I nearly offered him coffee and curled up on my chair, as if preparing for a chat with an old friend.

From the very first time I had seen Cedros, it was his unusual compassion that had made the difference in what would otherwise have been an uncomfortable encounter. He was coming, he said, to explore a long-standing conflict between his desire to be polygamous and his inability to live out the dream. He had in fact been in the same long-term relationship since he was twenty-one. He was thirty-eight now.

The first thing that struck me was Cedros's name, as I was unable to place it. Cedros was in fact American and his roots so complex, encompassing Mexico, Hungary and some Jewish ancestry, that he was in all honesty prepared to forget all about it, especially as he grew up in beautiful San Francisco, and this is where he met his first girlfriend and future wife. But all this mattered less than the fact, which I could still sense around him, that Cedros, unlike many who find their way to a private consulting room, began life from low down on the social scale. His mum was a Hispano, he said, and all the more honoured ancestry of his father's side meant very little till Cedros finally acquired his father's surname at the age of eight after much teasing at the rough state school that his mother, as a single parent, had no other option but to send him to. Looks didn't help much either, as these deprived beginnings in life were almost sculpted in the prematurely deep wrinkles on Cedros's forehead and the deeply set, closely spaced, dark eyes. Yet, it must have been the same compassion that made it work between us that had brought his current wife to him and kept her hooked for life – a Californian-raised hippy rich girl with some English heritage. She was his passport out of his past. It was not easy, he said, to transfer to England, but his specialty in geriatric nursing meant that he was much sought after and soon after his arrival a career nurse in the NHS.

So, to go back to compassion, I warmed to Cedros, in session one, as he was the only one of my patients in that very painful week to notice my discreetly bandaged ankle under my light late summer trousers and to give me advice about placing my leg high whenever I could. He spoke in a sweet manner that managed not to sound intrusive or overbearing. It is interesting what happens when the therapist who is supposed to 'see' things about the patient ends up feeling extraordinarily invisible, and his brief comment alleviated much of my resentment about working throughout the week with a swollen, sore ankle that none of my other patients seemed to care about or notice. Let alone that, as much as I try to avoid this, it is hard not to analyse myself, and spraining my ankle badly on my first week back at work after a long summer break was clearly suspicious. The other thing was that this was no ordinary summer at all, as it meant the end of the future I thought I had. Luke had broken the news that he wanted out and it did not matter at all that he called it a 'temporary break'.

But then, after this compassionate start, the difficult bits followed. Cedros had seen ten therapists in the space of two years, roughly one every two months with a break in between. The trigger was, he said, what happened before he left San Francisco, but the real issue that that incident brought up was his struggle with monogamy, or so he thought. The incident on its own was worth exploring, especially his take on it, but it was hard to get past the other stats, ten therapists in two years – I was number eleven and counting.

I no longer remember clearly which of the two, the incident that prompted his early departure or the number of therapists he had seen, was what we spent the most time on in that first session, but although by the end of it, I had offered him a second assessment, saying I was not convinced that it was right that we worked together, it was the fact that he noticed my ankle that broke the ice and my darker, suspicious thoughts.

The incident, as he presented it, was an inevitable blunder in his line of work, one that every senior nurse in an emergency unit would have made at some point, yet this one had cost him his mental health as well as his American licence to practise. The bottle from which he administered an injection was not fully labelled, and this was not unusual either, as this is how they arrived from the depot.

It was the task of the clinic's pharmacologist to classify them and label them for the staff, but this would sometimes take weeks, especially when they had a large order. The bottles would, in the meantime, be left stacked in the medicine cabinet. This was clearly underlying many of his issues, as I rushed to tell him; Cedros was a perfectionist and so, not wanting to delay a frail patient's dose, he chose to take medicine from the stack as the ready available ones for the unit had run out. It was the wrong dilution and, thankfully, it did not kill, but was enough to send the patient to ICU and Cedros to a tribunal. What made things worse was that he left the country before he needed to present himself to court, and that meant an automatic dismissal. The demons from his deprived past that the incident had unleashed were hard for him not to be driven by.

Cedros met his girlfriend in a private nursing home where he was a trainee and had become the favourite assistant of her wealthy Scottish grandfather who was close to death. From then on, it had been an upward career climb for him, having begun his PhD rather ironically in the ethics of geriatric nursing, when the disaster struck. Cedros felt that all the ugly class and race politics that his Democrat American friends pretended were nowhere near their friendship came back to hit him in the face during the weeks that followed his error. Even worse than that, he could have protected himself, he said, but he had readily presented himself to the ward nurse leader once he worked out what he had done, and it was probably because of his prompt timing that the life of the patient was saved.

I could see why this incident had been traumatic, I said in session one, but it was his frequent change of therapists that we needed to think about. What was it that he was trying to achieve, what was he unwittingly repeating through the comings and goings? And what about his attachment and the relationships with all these therapists? I did not of course get to see the parallel straight away, but when I had met Luke in my late thirties, we had talked at length about the fact that he could not settle before, he had gone through serial monogamy for a long time peppered with the occasional affair or one-night stand and, as I can now see clearly, monogamy had been an issue for Luke all along as much as it had been for Cedros. But Luke could not stop himself acting on the impulse, while Cedros could not bring himself to act on his desire, paralysed as it were by fear.

I had spent a long time talking through this issue with Luke in the early days. We had slept together already, but I was happy not to call it a relationship quite yet. I was trying to explain to him that I had no theoretical or ethical problem with polygamy or polyamory as it's become more trendy to call it nowadays, though the latter is even harder to digest, but once I was in a relationship with somebody I just could not handle emotionally the thought that they were sleeping around or even worse falling in love with somebody else. 'And given your history, how could I ever trust you?' I had asked him then after our second passionate night together. I still remember how close to tears I was. How embarrassed I felt that I could not handle a man as desirable as Luke and just enjoy the encounter. He persuaded me then that he was of course capable of feelings as deep as mine, and once he fell for somebody he would never hurt them through being dishonest. His previous girlfriends were different, not as sensitive as me, he had whispered that night, as he touched my cheek softly with the back of his hand and I felt then that he could see straight through me.

'Have you read *The Unbearable Lightness of Being*?' he had asked, and I was sent speeding downwards straight into the falling-in-love state.

'My favourite book ever', I had whispered back.

'You are like Tereza, you would just know if I were unfaithful, and I could never do that to you.'

'Do not underestimate me, Luke, I am not all that soft', I had teased him and pinched the tiny soft area of flesh round his waist. And yet, though I was right, my heart was not all that soft or else it would not have broken, he was wrong in the end. He had not been unfaithful, but he left me so that he could be.

I had been equally honest with Cedros in session two. I had felt moved by him and his story, yet, there was something unpalatable about being therapist number eleven. I did not tell him this of course in these exact words, and I could only hope he would not see how vulnerable I had been feeling and how I was not ready for yet another blow to my fragile ego. Had he explored before, I asked him, what it meant that he had seen all these therapists in a short period of time and what he kept going back to therapy for? It turned out that he had not been all that honest with all of them. Realistically, he said, it had only worked out with another two, and he could tell from the beginning that we would be a good match too.

'How come you did not stay for longer with the other two therapists it worked with then?' I asked him, and he shrugged his shoulders looking like a lost little boy.

'It just felt like a relationship had been formed with each of these therapists, and with another two before you, it was a good and genuine one, but with most of the other ones, it was not. It was still interesting nonetheless, I have to say, and I got a lot out of them despite our incompatibility. One thing I learnt through my experiences is that we develop through bad relationships almost as much as, if not more than, through the good ones, only though if we are strong enough to leave them in good time.'

'Yes, I can see that, but what prompted you to leave the therapists you felt compatible with? It sounds like you don't value attachment or the therapeutic relationship per se.'

'That sounds a bit judgmental', he had said non-defensively, and I cringed at the thought of how my anger about Luke's abandonment may have unwittingly crept into the room.

'I am just trying to understand you, Cedros', I answered, lowering my voice.

'It is just that it feels like it goes as far as it can with any given therapist within that time frame and then, I am ready to move on. Each of them has had a different perspective on me which I could learn from whether I agreed with it or not.'

I then decided to take him on and work within that time frame, being mindful in each session of how far we were in every given session from the two-month mark. It turned out that, not surprisingly, two months was a significant time frame too, as for the first two months of his life, Cedros had stayed with his mother in a home for young mothers when she was considering whether to give him up for adoption or not. Even more poignantly, in session three and while exploring this theme, Cedros told me that his mother, who had died rather young from throat cancer, as she'd been an avid smoker throughout her life, had talked to him on her sick bed, recalling the day she had made her decision.

'I love you, Cedros', she had said. 'I never regretted my decision to keep you, though I regret the life I had to have as a result. Aah, that fortune wheel never turned the other way for me, but it will for you, son, I can see it happening already.' This was the session during which Cedros wept woefully, as he had never done before in any of the other therapies, he said, and so, from then on, my anxiety that he would eject the therapy at the two-month mark dissipated, and though I counted the weeks diligently, I felt that we had established a true connection that would help him at last to let the past rest.

'I think, Cedros,' I had said calmly in that session, 'every time you leave a therapy at the two-month mark, you relieve your mother of the burden and responsibility of having to bring you up all by herself. In other words, it is like you also relieve yourself from some kind of existential guilt.'

So, in session nine, when Cedros sat comfortably on the chair across from me, it did not cross my mind that he may have any reason to keep repeating the past, until he said calmly, ten minutes into the session, that as he was sure I may have predicted, he was ready to move on, and this was going to be his last session.

The impulse was to slap him of course, especially as I knew straight away from the firm manner in which he spoke that the decision had been made and there was no point at all in trying to dissuade him. But the main reason I did not react at all was numbness, as in truth it was me who was being slapped for the second time in the space of two months. I remained very still and said very little throughout the session, as though neutrality and silence were the best punishment I could give him under the circumstances. Until, towards the end of the session, Cedros leant forward and said tenderly, as though comforting an upset child:

'It is not how you see it, Ellie', and I cringed hearing my name spoken so softly by him.

'It is not that I am caught up repeating something destructive or that I have not attached to you or that our relationship does not matter to me.'

'So? What is it like?' I mumbled and it was the best I could muster.

'Well ... It is like every time I repeat it, I understand it better and grow stronger through it.'

'Understand what?'

'My fear of polygamy. It is clearly a fear of abandonment, don't you think? That if I acted like I wanted, if I slept around, had affairs with other women, Faye would sooner or later find out and leave me. Ultimately, I cannot be myself with her, feeling too fragile to do what I want, to take the risk.'

'But you're not even sure it is what you really want, Cedros, like you're not that sure what you really want is to leave the therapy. What you are caught up in is trying to have the upper hand, to be the one who abandons rather than taking the risk of getting abandoned.'

'I trust that you can survive me leaving you, which makes it liberating to do what I want, and what I want, I think, is to try out what it feels like to have an intimate conversation with different people and to explore the limits of intimacy between us without getting hurt or abandoned, as you just said. Does this make sense?'

***

A few months later, my eye caught, in a newspaper that I found on my table at my local café, a story about a senior nurse at a private nursing home in Surrey who had administered a fatal dose to an old patient under suspicious circumstances. Throughout the day, I could not shake the dark thought that this could have been Cedros. Images of his wrinkle-sculpted face, his closely set eyes came through like in a nightmare, despite another part of me that held on closely to his tender voice, his thoughtful gestures and his incredible charm, the charm of being a man who cared.

Part III

Jake

> Jake is a psychoanalytic psychotherapist in his early forties. He runs a private practice from the front room of his Victorian house in north-west London. Jake connects deeply with his clinical work and his patients, he has an unconventional streak, and he is a risk taker. On the downside, he has a tendency to attempt to rescue his female patients, which makes him sometimes question his handling of the therapeutic boundaries. During these eight short stories, Jake's relationship with his partner, Isabel, goes into crisis through the birth of their first son. The threat of the loss of his relationship and the emotional alienation which comes to dominate his private life is in the background of the unfolding of these stories.

The crumpled coat

> This short story is about dissociation as a response to trauma. When loss and pain become too difficult to bear, the body takes over expressing what cannot be conceptualised in words. There is also a wider cultural context implicit here about the denial of feelings and vulnerability as a necessary condition for becoming a man. To the degree that one is willing to accept such a context as a given, such as in the example of young children being sent to boarding school and away from their parents and learning to see this as a privilege and not as a significant developmental trauma, it becomes very hard to make space for one's emotional reality and the integration of mind and body.

The first thing I noticed about him was his coat crumpled on the floor next to his chair like a curled-up foetus. Then, it was his accent, posh and clean like his freshly shaven face, as though he had just walked out of the shower, despite it being past 9 pm now.

'Thanks very much for seeing me so late', he said, but I could not feel the gratitude in the clean bell of his voice.

I nodded.

'Most therapists I called would not offer such late appointments.'

The floor lamp next to my chair dispersed a soft light in the room, the chequered blanket at the bottom of the couch looked even more cosy than usual. I liked working late, the quietness, the chance for contemplation, and then processing things in my sleep, the best place for the unconscious to begin unfolding.

'Do you always work long hours?'

He nodded. 'Very long indeed. Everyone knows that in my line of work, you do not stay around for long, unless you understand that this is the name of the game.' He stopped and looked around the room, discreetly, but his eyes like the eyes of the eagle were focused and efficient, 'I like it here. It seems like a predictable environment.'

'Predictable?'

'Yes, indeed. Again, I would not have survived in my line of work, if things were not predictable and organised in my mind. . . . Anyway, I did not come here to talk about work.'

98　The crumpled coat

'So, what brings you here?'

I now focused my eyes discreetly on him. It occurred to me that we seemed to make very similar use of gaze, focusing on a target, just at the right time, efficiently assessing what intervention, if any, was needed.

He leaned back, for the first time resting his head on the deliberately comfy backrest. He closed his eyes and from the slight fall of his chest, I could discern that he let out a discreet sigh. I waited. I could see the clock on the book shelf ticking quietly, ten minutes into the session. There was still plenty of time.

'I specifically wanted to see a male therapist.' His voice surprised me, as it came out while his eyes were still shut and his body still. 'This restricted my list even further. Male therapist, near the Jubilee line, so they can be reached easily on my way back from Canary Wharf and easy to find my way back home after the session. I wake up at 5 am every day you see, no time to waste. And somebody willing to offer very late appointments.'

'You seem to have thought very carefully about what commitment therapy would entail.'

'Naturally!'

'So, a female therapist was out of the question?'

'I am afraid my experience of women is that they are not predictable enough. It is biological logic really. Men follow timetables, women are driven by the moon. The two simply don't mix.'

I relaxed back in my chair too. I could see this was going to take a while. There was a sense of soothing in his dry discourse. A sense of coming back home.

'Are women not part of your life then?'

He leaned forward rather abruptly, opening his eyes and suddenly seeming very tired and mildly irritated. It was the first move that was not smooth, as though he was suddenly about to take my king away in a game of chess.

'Look, it is nothing to do with that. It is my body that brings me here. It is playing up and interrupting things. I am told it is psychological. To be frank, I don't care what it is. All I want is to sort it out.'

'Right. Can you tell me in what way your body is playing up?'

'I am afraid in the most ridiculous way one could imagine. I am in the middle of a Skype conference and my bowels take on a life of their own. I am determined to be on top of the situation, but no matter what I try, slow breathing, ignoring the excruciating pain in my stomach, focusing on something else, no matter what, I am overcome by cold sweat and, no matter what, everything turns into liquid inside me, it begins to literally pour out, and unless I get up and leave the room like a maniac without even having time to apologise for the interruption, the thing does not stop. A few times, I did not even make it to the toilet and I then had to leave work early altogether.'

I held my breath to suppress giggling. I felt a hint of panic surfacing. It would be totally inappropriate if I laughed or even smiled at this point. But come on, is that all it was? All this manic search for a male therapist near the Jubilee who could see him weekly at 9 pm, just because he was experiencing anxiety diarrhoea? The noise took me by surprise. It was like a wolf's wailing. Familiar and alien at the same time. I remembered witnessing this desperate sobbing once more recently, when my four-year-old, hopefully now securely snuggled up in his bed upstairs, fast asleep, had lost his security blanket, his very favourite soft blue teddy that his mum had brought him back from the airport the very first time she had left overnight, her treat for all the extensive breastfeeding as she called it. Although I could see that getting space away from a toddler felt at times very desirable, I really did not get it – how leaving him suddenly to spend a long weekend boozing with her girlfriends in Barcelona after two years of having him on her breast for what seemed like most of the time and never quite parting with him, had now become a treat.

He was curled up in the chair, his shoulders shaking violently. I extended my arm holding the box of tissues, but he did not make any eye contact. I discreetly left the box on the floor by his chair, hoping that he would locate it, if he needed to.

'I am sorry', I said quietly, feeling genuinely sorry for him now. He was a mess, a little helpless boy trapped in a grown man's body, determined to ignore and punish the little boy within.

'You don't understand', he said swallowing what sounded like snot. 'I have tried everything, a low fibre diet, an IBS control diet prescribed by a specialist gastroenterologist and followed to the letter, even a daily Imodium which made me terribly constipated, so much so, that I don't think my gut has any chance of ever recovering from it. In the end, it was the gastroenterologist who recommended analytic therapy. He said the bowel is a powerful organ and linked to our emotions and it seemed like my bowels were determined to tell me something. Such nonsense, yet I have no other hope left.'

'Richard,' I said leaning forward and trying to establish eye contact, 'you have given me many clues that you have very little belief that exploring your feelings may be helpful, yet there is a chance you may discover in the process of therapy that what felt like nonsense before begins to make some sense. From what you are saying, it seems like part of you is determined to sabotage what you value the most in your life, your career.'

'But why would I want to do that? I have worked so hard to be where I am, and people are relying on me. Why would I want to lose face like that?'

I sighed. This would be hard work. It felt like a heavy plinth had installed itself on my chest. 'People often come to therapy when they seem to want something, but another part of them will not let them have what they want, so they experience conflict.'

I looked at the clock. 9.31 pm. Less than twenty minutes left and it did not seem that we had got that far. 'I am aware of the time, Richard, and I would like to understand a bit more about you and your history before we have to conclude the session for today.'

He nodded. He seemed rather depleted now and ready to cooperate, like a toddler resting after a violent tantrum, during which he had almost turned blue through holding his breath.

'I would like to hear something about your background. What was your childhood like, your parents?'

'I think that I am a fairly easy person to read. Somebody trained like you should find it straightforward to guess what my childhood was like. I told you already, I thrive in predictable environments.'

I leaned back and felt the comfort of the cushioned chair on my back. Working late seemed such a good idea and, at times, as soothing as a crunchy cone of vanilla ice cream at the end of a sunny and windy afternoon by the beach just before dusk. It gave me the freedom to spend the afternoons with Jackson, take him to the park after I picked him up from nursery. It gave me and Isabel space to work out what was left of our relationship, her increasing absences, her preoccupation with work and her refusal to let me close, to admit that she was deeply disappointed by me. But now, after four early morning sessions and this being the third and last evening one, I could feel my achy back and feet, the dark side of the supposed freedom of my mid-afternoon run in the park, just before picking Jackson up from nursery.

'Did you go to boarding school?' I muttered.

He looked stunned. 'How . . . how did you guess?'

'You just told me that you are very predictable and that somebody like me should be able to guess what your childhood was like.'

I was aware of the faux pas, like pulling a party trick to impress my friends. I knew I did not need to show him how clever I was. What got into me?

'Well, I meant that you would guess that all was in order in my childhood. Things had to be a certain way and they always were. I learnt good table manners, solid routines, and yes, at the right time I was sent boarding.'

'What was that time, Richard?'

'Well, when school starts of course at the age of five. Reception.'

I felt a knot in my stomach. Here he was, a young five-year-old about to be abandoned by his parents and his bowels turning loose. The thought of Jackson going anywhere away from me . . . us would crumble me in seconds into a sorry wreck.

'This is very early to be sent away from home', I noted quietly.

Richard had now taken hold of a tissue and he was folding it neatly into increasingly smaller bright white squares, contrasting with the blue pinstripes of his suit trousers. He continued looking at his hand working quietly on the tissue in his lap for a while.

'You don't understand, boarding school was exactly like home. Very orderly, quiet and with huge opportunities for important learning, just less lonely than home. When Father took me, he patted me on the back and asked if I wanted to go home every weekend or just at the end of term, and I turned away from him and said: "Just end of term, Daddy. I think I will like it here." My father was a kind man, he made sure before he left that I knew I could write to him if I wanted to be picked up earlier and he would come and get me.'

'And your mother?'

In the silence that followed, I could hear my clock ticking loud, even though I, of course, use a completely quiet clock in my consulting room. I willed it to slow down and stretch the ten minutes of the session left for as long as possible, until I got that story right. My pulse was running fast.

'I have no recollection of my mother. She died when I was three and a half', he finally said.

I had unwittingly held my breath for so long during the silence that I was now panting. 'I am sorry to hear that, Richard.'

'As I said, I have no recollection of my mother', he repeated, every single word sounding like an ice cube falling on the hard metal surface of a sink.

'Richard, we only have five minutes left before the end of the session, but I feel that we are on to something important here. Could you try and tell me if you have any memory at all from around the time of your mother's death either before or after?'

Why was I rushing him? What was I trying to achieve? It was not good technique to get a new patient I knew nothing about to reveal sensitive information right at the end of the session. Surely, he would come back? What else could he do? He seemed desperate to get a hold of himself. The fear had crept back in; I imagined walking out of the session into the living room. Would Isabel be there waiting for me, asking how my new session went? She used to be fascinated by my work, and I made a point of telling her earlier that I was seeing a new patient tonight, somebody who sounded posh and mysterious. I could already anticipate the sinking feeling in my heart, if it turned out that the lights were off and she was curled up on her side of the bed, with her back turned, her copper waves spreading like rust on her pillow between us, drifting us further apart. It suddenly occurred to me, how could somebody as distinctly cold as Richard ever feel cosy and familiar, like going back into an empty house with nobody to greet me; like the house of my adolescence, of my mother's oblivious withdrawal into her gin and tonics.

'I only remember the hospital really', he said so quietly that I could barely hear him.

'The hospital where your mother died?'

'Yes, no, you don't understand. I didn't know she had died, neither did my father. I had high fever, vomiting, diarrhoea. I had lost a lot of fluid and I was becoming lethargic. I don't remember any of that of course. This is what I was told. My father said he and the nanny they had employed while my mother was in hospital were worried about me. They thought I was becoming dehydrated.'

Even in the dim light of my consulting room, I could see that his previously pale face was flushed now, his light-blue eyes like the sky over ice in Alaska were shiny. He talked quickly, feverishly, and I struggled to keep up.

'All I remember is the nurse room where they finally took me. By the time we were there, I was a mess, I was not able to hold it in the car, I remember the awful smell of vomit on my hair and a nurse trying to put a nappy on me rather harshly, saying I was a big boy now, I should not have to need one. Then my father went to check on my mother. We lived in a small town, this was the only hospital we could reach within reasonable time. She had been there for three days, complicated labour. I don't remember any of that of course. . . .. But I remember my father coming back to find me and talking to the nanny quietly. Then she gave a high shrill and covered her face. And that was it, my father was reduced to a wreck, he was rocking back and forward, sobbing quietly, staring at the void. It was as though I was not there.'

'What happened to your mother, Richard?' I said, trying to talk steadily despite the strangling knot in my throat.

'She gave birth to a dead foetus. She was exhausted, trying to give birth over three nights yet refusing to go under. She had had a very normal birth with me apparently and she believed she could do it. She then bled a lot. They tried to save her, but it was too late. When my father walked in, she had just died and they were about to contact him. Apparently, he refused to see the baby, a girl, which meant that he could not go near her either, as the last thing she had said was that she wanted to be buried with her baby daughter in her arms. All he could see, he said to me much later on, was a bundle of ginger curls in her arms. Those two wanted to go together, no space for anyone else.'

He took a deep breath in and looked at me as though we were about to conclude our business meeting. 'Is it time?' he said.

Life's meaning

> Psychoanalysis has based the idea of psychic development on achieving separation and individuation, and more specifically separation from the mother. The relationship with one's mother is also often at the core of gaining insight into what has gone wrong and has led to symptoms of mental distress. The mother-daughter relationship in particular is considered within most psychoanalytic writing as fraught and complex, as it is on the basis of identification or disidentification with the mother that female identity is built. In this short story, Layla, one of the teenagers from Part I, is visiting a therapist in order to come to terms with her complicated relationship with her mother, which one could say is driven by unhealthy attachment and role reversal. What is being reconsidered here is the parameters of what a good enough life for an adult is, and how one is to deal with this most enduring of attachments, that with one's own mother.

'It was yet another one of these weeks', she said. 'You know, the "nothing much happening" weeks.' She smiled her witty smile and, as always, her slightly crooked teeth made her face look light and cheerful.

We were sat facing each other at an angle, both cross-legged and as usual Layla's face, when smiling, had the same effect on me: it put me in a good mood. A good mood that I knew fully well was unjustified, as by now I was familiar with what exactly 'nothing much happening' meant. That other than going to work, she spent the whole week doing nothing much else than taking care of her mother.

Layla had come to see me a year ago, when her mother, having recently been diagnosed with MS, had moved in with her. Her parents had suffered a bitter and unhappy marriage, marked by racial friction in a city in the North of England where they all lived. It was a case of, as Layla had told me several times already, divorce being much more liberating and life-giving than the limbo the whole family endured. Layla's father was Moroccan, one of a small minority of immigrants from that part of the world to the North of England. Her mother on the other hand was brought up locally in another unhappy family set-up, and as much as she saw Layla's father as her passport to escaping a childhood and a town that she loathed, the romance did not last long enough to make her forget that, geographically at least, she was still stuck in the same place. Still, Layla's birth was one of the last romantic times in her parents' relationship. The romance dissipated soon after, when the realities of child-rearing hit home. While still in a trance-like state of being in love (and lust perhaps as well), Layla's mother consented to giving her first daughter a provocatively Arabic name that would turn heads in the local community. Layla said that it was only upon moving to London that she came to appreciate her name and not to feel deeply embarrassed by it.

In fact, if I am honest, I still remember clearly how surprised I was to first meet Layla when she had referred herself to me. It was not just having an Arabic name, but her surname was exotic-sounding as well, and so in the first ten minutes of the session, in a state of bewilderment, I had wondered silently if I had got her details wrong. Layla seemed to me a typical Londoner in both looks and manners, with her straightened sharply cropped hair, casually smart work attire, fast talking, partying often with her friends and working long hours. She only occasionally finished a sentence with a hint of a Northern accent, which gave me a clue that she had not been brought up in London. She told me later on that she had considered changing her surname and taking on her mother's maiden name, but she could not bring herself to do it, as she could imagine the hurt she would cause her father. I was not surprised to hear that, as she was a strange combination of somebody determined to break free, which had driven her to a social work college in outer London in her late teens, and yet, equally determined not to displease either of her parents, an almost impossible endeavour, as they hardly ever saw eye to eye.

Layla's birth was followed by the quick succession of two other more complicated and even traumatic births which made Layla's mother decide to become one of the few women of her generation willing to try the pill. Not that she needed to for long, Layla added, as her parents' relationship disintegrated so much more that, by the time she was going to school, they had moved to separate bedrooms, leaving the three children to squeeze into the third bedroom of their semi-detached house. The fact that her parents stressed to her that she had the privilege of owning an adult-sized single bed in the room while her brothers had to make do with dwarf-length bunk beds for years to come was little consolation for the violation of her privacy that she reported to me, as one of the main unpleasant features of her childhood. She was not one to demand things, but thankfully by the time she was twelve her father decided to move to the living room and to make a point of giving his tiny bedroom to her. He occupied the large sofa in the living room, watching TV there in the evening with the door closed, which made her mother seethe, and leaving home very early for his thankless job in the nearby electrical appliances factory the following morning. But even after Layla finally acquired her own bedroom, her mother always found many uses for Layla's eagerness to help, which meant that she would spend most of her time doing chores for her mother, and only use her room for sleep.

Layla had a strange effect on me since the beginning. She reminded me of some of the best years of my life, sixth form. It was then that I had finally gone back to the freedom of a mixed state school, I hung out with girls, flirting, partying, not quite committing to anything more serious yet. Girls were my friends and, as friends, we would get on well, have fun together. It was romantic relationships that spoiled things, as I was to discover later on. Layla could have easily been one of these girls. She was pleasant, friendly, considerate and fun at the same time. She had a dry humour that as much as I tried (as I knew it concealed feelings that were not funny at all), I found it hard not to respond to. Before she had embarked on becoming her mother's main carer, which was the very thing that had driven her to therapy, Layla had lived a life reminiscent of my sixth-form years.

'I do friendship, but no romance, just sex', she told me smiling in the first session. 'What we call nowadays friends with benefits.'

This encapsulated rather well Layla's views on relationships.

'I just don't fancy the roller-coaster of romance that ends invariably in heartache.'

Instead, she dated some of the more handsome boys her friends fancied, but, as she put it, she sent them home if she felt that they came anywhere close to falling in love with her. In truth she was cynical at heart.

Layla's lightness in the sessions was rather strange as her present life circumstances could not be described as light by any means. In her mid-thirties now, she had grown tired of partying, she said, and she found it a much more worthwhile endeavour to take care of her mother's deteriorating condition. As she put it, if she did not, nobody else would. It was not that her mother's physical state was currently so extreme, though significant loss of vision and dizzy spells had made her rather unsteady on her feet. Her mother's behaviour towards her on the other hand was totally unreasonable and was becoming worse by the day. This was what brought her to therapy. The question of how much it was fair to tolerate. This was also strange in another way, as rather than being pushed to the limit by what was clearly intolerable behaviour towards her, she was rather asking the question theoretically. She was a cool customer indeed! Or at least, she seemed to be.

Layla's cynicism seemed to derive much from her social work career.

'Once you have been into enough council flats in hard-core inner-city estates and have seen enough men hold their little daughters supposedly tenderly on their laps with an erection under their tracksuits in full view, trying to persuade you that *all is well, love,* giving you the signal at the same time that your life might be at risk if you dare take a step in further than their threshold, believe me, once you witness this scene enough times, you lose any faith in romance.'

Though it was now a year ago, I remembered clearly these early conversations with Layla and her view that focusing on giving her mother a better life than that she'd had up to now was perhaps the only cause she could be less cynical about. I also still remember vividly the moment in our first session when she told me about her mother's disclosure which, in my view, spread the seeds of cynicism, even before she embarked on becoming a social worker.

'I was just about to turn twelve when my mother told me that she was adopted', Layla said. 'It was one of these moments, you know, when everything falls into place at once. All her pervasive unhappiness made sense at last. And yet, what's hard to digest is that people adopt children and end up abusing them as well. She never told me the details of that, but she said enough for me to get the hint. She gave me a clear message that all men want from you is sex and there is no goodness in it or in them. They are best avoided at all costs.'

Layla saw as a developmental achievement, and I had to agree with her on that, conquering sexuality as pleasant and fun in her adult life. And yet, it was precisely that aspect of her life, the partying, the boyfriends, that she had decided to give up on in order to take care of her mother.

It occurred to me that Layla and I had this in common: mothers who needed us to rescue them and take care of them and give their lives meaning. As much as I was always willing to do that for my own mother while she was around and the guilt for not managing to save her lingered for years after her death, driving me to therapy in the end, I could feel that the mission Layla had undertaken to make her mother happy was utterly unrealistic and a possible psychic death for her. At times, I thought that I should have more sympathy for Layla's mother, as she had had a hard life after all, but I was rarely suspicious of the hateful indignation I felt rising in me every time Layla reported an incident of her mother's utterly outrageous prima donna-like outbursts.

Our session last week, which she began by reporting that nothing much had happened, was one of many with a similar opening after which Layla had proceeded to narrate a number of instances during the week when she had tried to entertain her mother, to take her out to a fancy restaurant or for a coffee in a special place over the weekend or for a slow walk by the river, holding her hand at the same time to make sure she felt safe. Her mother had invariably managed to turn the outing into a disaster. She complained about the weather, the restaurant service or developing a new worrying symptom on the spot. No matter how many times I had responded with pointing out that Layla needed to set boundaries and asking her why she had invited this into her life, and whether this was the only kind of intimacy she could possibly have, my comments did not seem to make much difference at all. Just before she arrived for the session, it occurred to me that, perhaps, her relationship with her mother was the only one in her life in which Layla allowed herself to be romantic. I thought this might provide us with a breakthrough or at least the chance for exploration.

I took the opportunity of the familiar opening to suggest to Layla that she was in fact right, nothing much was happening in her life. She was trying to help her mother live her own life instead and not with much success either.

'I don't understand what's wrong with that', she said, and I sensed an unfamiliar edge in her tone. 'Would I be better off trying to help a stranger become my boyfriend and live his life?'

'But this would be your life as well. You would get things you would want for yourself through that.'

'Like?'

'Like fun, intimacy, children perhaps?'

'I have made a firm decision on that. Too much trouble and heartache. I don't do heartache, remember?'

Her familiar, witty smile was back and I can't pretend I did not feel a huge sense of relief to recover the feeling of lightness.

'I don't know if you have realised this, but I am the only person my mother has ever been intimate with. This is why she is difficult, she doesn't have to pretend with me, she can be herself.'

'And you?'

'I guess I am myself too. Showing her that I love her, that I want to be there for her. She will never have anyone else in her life who will do that for her.'

'But isn't that through her own choice?'

It was one of these frustrating instances during a therapy session when a conversation that made perfect sense to the therapist did not seem to move the patient even an inch. After she left, I could not shake the feeling of being incompetent for hours to come.

***

On Monday morning, two days after our next session was due, I received a note from Layla. It was polite, but cold. She said we seemed to have been stuck on familiar ground for a while now, but in fact, rather surprisingly, our last session made it crystal clear to her that she was on the right path for what she wanted from life. For that, she had to thank me, she wrote, for being such a spirited and challenging interlocutor.

My first reaction upon receiving Layla's note was anger. I felt used. I thought I had contained all her repressed feelings of rage and frustration towards her mother and now she was walking out on me, leaving behind all her toxic waste. Was she treating me like one of her ex-boyfriends, I wondered, because I dared as much as to care for her and like her? Yet, Layla's last words that she was the only person in her mother's life who would ever care for her and love her stayed with me, and made me wonder for days to come about life's meaning.

Three in bed

> One of the themes in this short story is how in cross-cultural relationships, cultural traits become ways to represent psychic obstacles, which sometimes takes the form of stereotyping the other. In this sense, culture, like other symbolic representations, can stand for a third element in a relationship. For some couples, introducing such a third element in their relationship can be necessary in order to achieve intimacy. It is like jouissance only becoming a possibility when a child realises that he/she is not the only object of the mother's desire. This story also suggests that, in couples therapy, there are at least two, if not more, couples in the room, the couple seeking therapy and the therapist's internal representations of what a couple is.

'I cannot stand living in suspicion for the rest of our lives together' was the reason Jack had given for seeking out couples therapy, unusual as it was for the man in a couple to be the one who thought therapy was the answer. Jack was in his early fifties and Mikiko about a decade younger. As is often the case with South East Asian women, it was hard to tell her age. This had a significant effect on me as, since seeing them for the first time, I could not help shake off the thought that Jack fell neatly into the stereotype of the middle-aged Westerner seeking young Asian women for sexual exploitation. It did not help that he insisted that the silly text he had sent to an unknown Facebook friend meant nothing, while Mikiko directed her gaze absently outside the window every time he mentioned it, as though she wanted to fly out, not to be there and be faced with the hurt of his indiscretions. He was chubby and businessman-like in all his demeanour, she was petite and pale. They were unmistakably the archetypical father–daughter couple.

Seeing couples is something that comes to me naturally. Although I was raised by a single mother, my grandparents were a model of normality throughout my childhood. Therapy somewhat changed the rosy image I had of them, as surely, if they were all that good, my mother would not have ended up single for most of her adult life and dying of alcoholism almost as soon as she saw me off to university. Yet, even back then, they were my main support network I could fall back on, and my surviving their only daughter's early death made them even more determined to stand by me.

She wanted a baby, Mikiko would say, it was her last chance. He would not do that, he would assert, until their relationship improved. He was not a sperm machine, besides – as she knew already, he had two adult children from a previous relationship. Yes, but she had none, she would utter quietly, her words enveloped in the silk of her voice. How much rage was behind the girl voice, the soft, quiet tone? Well, if they improved the sexual part of their relationship, which had suffered hugely since she saw the text, maybe having a baby would sort itself out, he would say. He was not that good at contraception anyway. But as things stood, they hardly saw each other, let alone become intimate. If he told her he would have a baby with her she would get intimate, she would offer; if she told him she wanted to be intimate, he would consider a baby, he would reply. It went round and round.

I wondered what the text said, and if it was the only sign of Jack's infidelities. I could not shake the image from my head of him using internet porn, young Japanese women in awkwardly humiliating positions. I would imagine again and again Mikiko checking out his computer in silence after he fell asleep, spending time looking at the images one by one, then switching it off quietly, sleeping on the other side of the bed with her back turned to him, setting off for work early before he was up the following morning. She was an estate agent promoting Japanese properties in London, her work required regular travelling to Japan, it made her as scarce as she could be in order to manage Jack and the hurt their relationship caused her.

I was aware the text had become the elephant in the room. I wanted to ask what it said and to whom, yet every time Jack mentioned it, Mikiko's gaze focused outside the window and gave me a sense that she would flee the room. 'Was there sexual innuendo in the text?' I had dared to ask her. 'No!' Jack protested, 'it was just a friendly text to a lady I don't even know.' 'Quite! That's even worse', Mikiko spoke up at last. 'Why would you send friendly messages to ladies you don't know?' 'Well, maybe if you spent more time with me, I would have less time to be on Facebook.' He had a point there, I had to admit.

We were a smug couple, Isabel and I, in the early days. After an intense session in bed, we would talk about the 'fakies', even spend time in bed impersonating them and giggling so much that in the end, we would hold our stomachs in pain. 'Honey, would you have some coffee with me?' 'I am busy painting my nails darling!' we would in chorus mock a British couple we had met on a recent holiday in Tuscany, who seemed to live two planets apart facing in opposite directions, so much so that the man had latched on to us desperately on the lookout for some company. 'Poor darling, he is so talkative and after a month of settling into our villa here in Tuscany, he is desperate for some friendly conversation in his native language. You guys must come round for dinner, though I don't do cooking, but we have discovered a fantastic deli with local products nearby!'

'I still remember,' Isabel had said, putting her leg over my hips, 'I still remember how much you blushed when you tried to refuse them in your polite British middle-class way. You looked as red as a lobster.'

I registered the soft inside of her knee lying on the outside of my leg. She often took that position when she was turned on, in the mood for sex.

'And where do you come from, Mrs?' I pinched her bottom.

'Do you remember her name? Poppy? Gosh, Poppy was such a bimbo!'

'No, she was a case of a proper girl, a boarding school girl whose parents had found her a good catch mature boyfriend.'

'Come on, Jake, you always romanticise women.'

She rode me now sitting provocatively on my lower belly. She was only wearing some soft cotton knickers and a logo black T-shirt like she always did in bed back in the days of living in her flat in Notting Hill. Her ginger hair fell in soft curls around her face. 'Bimbo!', 'Boarding school!', 'Bimbo!', 'Boarding school!' The rest faded. As our entanglement progressed, other faculties than memory took over.

But it was a long ago since sexual energy was live between us, and while sitting with Jack and Mikiko, I knew exactly what it felt like to have entered a period of drought, not knowing when, or if, the atmosphere will moisten up ever again.

Mikiko and Jack had met in Japan some ten years ago. It was one of Jack's grand business plans shortly after his divorce that had brought him to Tokyo. He had fallen in love with the city, he said, even before he had met Mikiko, who was senior PA to one of the business consultants he had visited while there. His plans to introduce the Japanese tea ceremony to certain five star hotels in London had fallen through, as even Japanese tea could not compete with the English high tea, whose oriental origins should not have been forgotten, Jack stressed as part of his advertising campaign. But it was in fact an idea that Mikiko ended up using to work her way up one of the most prestigious Japanese estate agencies in London. She liaised with her boss in Tokyo to create the heart of the home around tea drinking in Japanese properties in Mayfair that she proved excellent at promoting.

To start with, Mikiko had said in one of the first sessions, Jack was like any other Westerner she had ever met, a bit overweight, which I gathered was her polite way of meaning rather obese, and in awe of a culture he did not truly understand. She had been given the task by her boss to take him round and introduce him to Japanese culture. What made her fall for him was how quickly he took to complex aspects of the Japanese way of life that she introduced him to. He was a natural with food and, within a week, he was ordering for himself like a Japanese man, with the help of her translation. He was also fiercely romantic and proper and when at the end of the week he asked her to come and live with him in London, he had not as much as kissed her or held her hand, Mikiko said.

Mikiko and Jack married in a traditional Japanese Buddhist ceremony about a year after she had moved to London with him, attended by Jack's two university-age sons who had by now also been converted to Mikiko's cooking, and her parents who took their only trip to London for the occasion.

All couples are like cross-cultural marriages, it occurred to me in session three. When it works, each person grows, living in the other's culture like an anthropologist transforming themselves during fieldwork in a remote place.

When it starts falling apart, it feels more like being trapped in a West African village struck by Ebola into quarantine. When Jackson was born, it felt like my relationship with Isabel changed from being a mutual exchange of culturally diverse delights to living together in the Ebola village with no escape route. Not that this had entirely sidelined my excitement about becoming a father, but Isabel's fright and claustrophobia were hard to miss. Should I have suggested that she sought help for postnatal depression then, when she was clearly at the worst of it? Did I miss the boat for ever by hoping that we could pull through this together? Seeking help, this is what Jack and Mikiko were doing now, and even though it may not have seemed like a big thing to them, it may be what makes the difference in the end.

Jack and Mikiko both grew in each other's company during the first few years of their relationship. He lost weight naturally with no diet at all, just by following the Japanese way of eating, Mikiko informed me. As for her, she was accustomed to being the only child of older parents with chronic health problems. Deciding to come to London at the spur of a moment was a life-changing event. She realised how fiercely independent and proud she really was. She quickly found herself a highly paid job in the estate agency and grew her network of friends. For the first time ever, she felt in charge of herself.

What changed everything was Mikiko's mother's death three years ago, Jack said. As usual when a difficult subject was being touched on, Mikiko grew silent, withdrawn. Her mother suffered from congenital heart disease which meant that her pregnancy with Mikiko was high risk. It didn't help that both her parents were heavy smokers.

'It must be difficult for you that your father now lives in Tokyo by himself', I had intercepted. 'Does he have any other family nearby?'

'Not much. Just his sister, but she lives two hours away by train.'

'Are you worried about him?'

'I try not to think about it', she said in a flat tone.

'Do you blame me for taking you away from your country, your parents?' Jack came in.

It struck me that as much as Jack was emotionally articulate, his openings always had the same effect of closing things down between them.

'Not at all', Mikiko replied sharply, eyes focused outside the window.

'See', Jack turned to me. 'I try to talk to her and I just can never reach her. When we come here and she reacts like this, I end up thinking that there is no point.'

'Jack, it strikes me that you do try to reach out as you just said, but you want Mikiko to react in the way that you deem appropriate. Then, by talking to me about her while she is present, it is like you are blocking her out, which is effectively giving her back what you feel you are getting from her. Maybe Mikiko means what she just said to you at face value, she does not blame you for being away from her parents, she feels grateful to you for this.'

I noticed Mikiko's eyes become teary and I paused.

'It is like your Japanese tea business idea, Jack', she said in an unusually clear voice. 'You wanted to persuade British hotels that tourists would come to London to enjoy Japanese and not English tea. You thought they didn't get you, but in fact, you didn't get them. You can never see things my way either. I sometimes wonder why you bothered marrying somebody from another culture.'

'Meaning? What's your way?' he muttered impatiently.

'Of course, I worry about my father, but to be honest, he is just like me, fiercely proud and independent. He would not let me help him out even if I was there. It is wounding my own pride I blame you mostly for.'

He shifted uncomfortably. He sighed and waited, but no more was coming. I breathed, as I realised that like Jack, I was holding my breath for more.

'What are you talking about?' he said after a while.

'You don't even know where to look, Jack, to find original Japanese pornography. What you are watching is just rubbish. Tacky, just like you are becoming!'

Jack had been reluctant to talk much about his background before that session where Mikiko confronted him with what she knew to be the case. Any of my questions about his history were rebuffed with *happy, loved-up family, parents close to each other, two older sisters who mothered Jack as well.* I was surprised to find out six months into our work together, after the session when Mikiko let him know that she knew exactly what he was up to, that Jack had gone to boarding school from the age of seven. He was not a planned baby, he admitted, and his parents found it hard to cope with the burden of an extra child who happened to be a boisterous boy as well. Jack admitted that in many ways, it had felt like his parents had sent him away while the four of them continued being the family before he had unexpectedly disturbed their equilibrium.

It felt like boarding school was the key to understanding their relationship. It did not take much for Jack to feel rejected. When Mikiko's mother died, he secretly wondered if she had regretted following him to London. She had made a bunch of Japanese friends here, but she had hardly bothered to open up to anyone else, and while before he had felt honoured to be inducted into her culture, it now felt more like he was once more the odd one out. The more rejected he felt, the more he took solace in solitary pursuits involving various degrees of daydreaming. And the more he did so, the more distant Mikiko grew.

***

The end of couples therapy is much easier to discern than in individual work. Mikiko and Jack continued coming to see me for another six months. While in the sessions they continued to fight and explore some of the same problems that had brought them to therapy, I knew when they had arrived from hearing whispering and giggles outside my door for a couple of minutes before the bell rang. Sometimes, I would grow paranoid and wonder whether they were having a laugh at me before they walked in. Indeed, one time, they confirmed that they were talking about my plant with the red fruits in the front yard, wondering if I liked to eat them. 'Or perhaps, to share them with my lover!' Mikiko chipped in and they both burst out laughing.

In that session in early June, Mikiko was particularly radiant and for the first time I noticed that she was a grown woman rather than a little girl in trendy clothes. The giggling continued for a while, and then Jack said they had an announcement to make. Mikiko was pregnant and though for some reason they tended to argue every time they came to see me, things between them were now better than ever before.

'If I am honest, there was another area of big concern for me that I had not even dared to bring here, partly not to upset Mikiko even more, and partly as I didn't know if it was an area you dealt with. I was afraid you may refer us to a specialist, if I did.'

'In other words, you were scared that I would send you away, Jack, right?'

'Right!' he smiled.

'Sex had never really worked between us and now that I know how things can be different, I can tell you for sure that it was really not working before.'

'Yes, it was my fault. I thought this is how it is for the woman, something that just men like really.'

'But . . .' Jack said, sending Mikiko a hesitant look to get her approval.

'But, I like inducting people into my culture. This is something I am good at. And I thought I may as well introduce Jack to proper Japanese pornography, which is not forbidden or shameful in Japan like pornography is seen here, it is a form of art really. And it produced results. We are loved-up and I am pregnant!'

'And may I say, that it was now my chance to introduce Mikiko to the pleasures of sex, even if with the help of her own culture.'

It occurred to me that two in bed is not always a satisfying premise. For some couples, like Isabel and me, it is the only way it can ever work. For others, like Mikiko and Jack, a third party of some sort is the royal route to climax. They need a benign figure, either in the form of a therapist or an inductor of some sort to hold their hand and guide them. It seemed that they had now found this third party right in the middle of their bed.

Driven

> This story is about grief. It is tempting to think, as some theories in psychotherapy suggest, that grief is a process including stages, which lead to recovering and resuming one's life. While this may be true to an extent, there is a more philosophical question about the unbearable nature of grief, when the person lost to us is inextricably woven into the fabric of our psyche. How can one ever recover from losing a life companion, a key figure from one's childhood or a child? This story is about the strong urge to be attached and to hold on to our affectionate attachments, which most of us experience as intimate parts of ourselves.

'My daughter thinks I should come here', my new 3 pm patient, called Alice White, says, and a laugh sticks in her throat, as she crosses her slender, long legs.

The clock reads 3.01 pm. I always find it hard to concentrate for the first ten minutes of a session. My mind jumps, butterfly-style, from the aftertaste of my lunch, to the latest email, with an edge, I have received from my training institution, to Isabel and what she might be doing right now, and whether she may ever be thinking of me.

The woman across from me seems unpleasant from her tone of voice, yet my gut feeling says that the session will go fast, like a speedy car, and that the less I say, the faster it will glide as on a smooth driveway. She would be at home in a convertible indeed, her tousled short hair is layered expertly at an alternative coiffeur's in Soho, the grey cleverly concealing the blended-in colour. She wears transparent round glasses with a sharp pink hue on their two edges, asymmetrical clothes, falling graciously on her svelte frame. Best of all, she has a singer's throaty voice. Even better, she doesn't attempt to conceal from me that she has an adult daughter with high opinions, always a sign of true confidence in a woman.

'You seem to fit the stereotype of the silent therapist, not saying much.'

'It depends. I guess I have a feeling you may be helped more without the interference of my biased questions.'

'Such as?'

'Such as, why your daughter thinks you need to have therapy and why you think you don't.'

She laughs throwing her head backwards. 'I think I like you', she says, clearing a wet cough at the same time as speaking.

She puts me in a good mood, rare at the beginning of a session, especially when the session is number one, when nearly everybody arrives drowning in despair and at the height of existential anxiety about having taken a wide step out onto the precipice, into a therapist's room. There is something wholesome about her, something that perhaps, as she rightly hinted, will not necessitate an intervention.

'As you may guess from my hoarse voice, I am a smoker. A very measured one, I've got to say though. I smoke a lot some days, less others, none at all for weeks. But I never quit, I just part with my fags temporarily, knowing that the pleasure will be back in my life one day soon.' She stops and strokes the grey velvet arm of the chair in an almost explicitly sexual way. 'Do you think this is a problem?' she says focusing her gaze on me.

This woman is fun, unusual, playful. She asks me questions I have no idea how to answer, yet I am more than willing to try. I wish I could have this kind of fun back with Isabel. . . . I gently brush the thought away, almost as sensually as her hand lying on the arm of my client chair. For the first time in a long time, I feel a glimpse of hope that intimacy with Isabel may even be possible again one day.

'Maybe the question is not as much if your smoking is a problem per se, but what it represents.'

'Meaning?'

'Well, it may be a more interesting question to ask what is it of your experience and feelings that you symbolise through choosing to smoke in this way. Is this why your daughter wanted you to see a therapist?'

'Well, she is upset that I am smoking. I had stopped over fifteen years ago. She hardly remembers me holding a fag as, when she was old enough to ask questions, this is when I quit. But what she remembers clearly is her dad chain-smoking throughout her childhood. And then, dying of it.'

Suddenly, she is up, pacing up and down in front of my bay window, which takes me rather by surprise.

'Are you all right?' I say, leaning forward.

She tries to peep outside the window, but the white wooden shutters at the bottom are, as usual, closed. As she goes on tip-toe to look out through the top part of the window, she looks like a trapped gazelle.

'Look, can I have a fag? I know I really sound like an addict now, but can I quickly pop out at your front yard for a cigarette? I will only take three minutes.'

Right at this moment, it is tempting to join her in her crazy dance, to tell her/show her/be with her in all the unbearable feelings I am having as much trouble as her holding down without collapsing. I feel the urge to get up as well and join her faster and faster steps, but in the end, it is my stillness, my steady weight on the therapist's chair that I think helps her to return to hers and to start at last the fluid, fluent talking I had anticipated from the beginning of Alice's journey into her feelings.

She seems completely oblivious to her tears rolling steadily down her cheeks, as she paints in every detail one of the most delicious love stories that has ever entered my consulting room. It is only my fear of her regretting the potential mess her tears have left on her make-up or clothes or both that prompts me to interrupt her flow to pass her the tissues sitting on the table between us. Fear never works well in sessions, as when I pass her the tissues, she looks at me with eyes wide open and says, 'I can't believe I have told you so much!'

Alice met her husband at university, studying journalism. He came from a wealthy, highbrow Indian background, desperate to escape it despite the privilege. She was a true representative of the English middle class, she said, both her parents were teachers, no money, just culture, and manners of course. It was a case of opposites attract. They fell hard and fast for each other, testing each other as well of course. For her, the fear of truly falling for somebody meant defiance and playing hard to get, letting him think that she was dating other men, when she could not even bring herself to snog somebody in one of the wild seventies parties she used to go to with all her left-wing hippy friends. For him, it was coming to accept and to respect her ways, ways so different from what women were meant to be in his background that had made all the difference. Cigarettes and writing was what brought them together, and reading too. Sometimes, they did all these things together and making love of course, often all three or four of these activities at once. And then, their daughter, Alaina, came rather early, the result of failed contraception. A beautiful name I thought, blending the syllables together in sonorous harmony,

'Just one?' I ask. 'No more children?'

'To be honest, we had to face up to it. There was no space between us for more, it was just too busy with our being together. And Alaina, in the unique way only children can, managed to find her place between us and to be close to both, although secretly more to her dad, I think, like girls often are.'

By this time in the session, she is toying with a cigarette in her hands, holding it, passing it from one hand to another, occasionally putting it between her lips, leaving a slight wet mark on it, I imagine. Again, it is not hard to sense sexual innuendo in all these gestures, and yet, it is Alice's mind that is smoothly occupying the room and the gliding motion of the story, like the convertible on a fast motorway I had imagined from the beginning.

Alice and her husband, Avi, worked as journalists for a number of years, but in the end, it was their love of reading that won through. They devoured literature together. Books stacked the floor on the two sides of their snug bed and swapped sides with no exception. Their literary agency was well known and established, I was made to understand, and it also stood for the rich left literary tradition in Islington where they built their home.

'Alaina is also working in the agency', she says. 'I know we are a bit insular as a family, I mean we all love to spend time with each other and by ourselves, but we have some pretty darn good friends as well.'

'It was Alaina who spotted it', she says, after a brief silence of holding the creased cigarette in her mouth. 'The lump on her father's neck. It kind of bothers me it was her, as we have always been so physical, so close, you know? A hard, small lump on the side of his neck, like a shrivelled chickpea. It just went downhill from then on.' No words for a while, just the early November sunset sending sideways rays through the top window of my Victorian front reception, and the cigarette in her hand rolling and rolling.

'What is the cigarette doing for you?' I say softly, taking the risk of breaking the rich silence.

She seems oblivious that she is holding it at all, and looks at me with the same wide eyes I had noticed earlier when she was pacing up and down looking outside the window. They were startled eyes, it occurs to me now, which had not become used yet to the sight of death.

'I just wanted to suggest', I say in a voice as low as possible in order to still be heard clearly, 'that holding on to this cigarette right now, and the stopping, bingeing or light smoking or whatever else you do with cigarettes, is a way of holding on to Avi. The cigarette is almost like Avi is in the room with us right now.'

She looks at me, and keeps looking and looking, saying nothing.

I like Alice. I can imagine sitting across from her at the kitchen table reading books, nursing a steaming cup of coffee, exchanging words, which we both know what they mean, turning the pages almost together, building the everyday music of intimacy.

She goes on for a while talking about Avi's deteriorating body and sick bodies in general, how they take over when it comes to illness, how they slowly separate from their owners and how they become the thing demanding centre stage. It was unbearable to watch it, she says, and as the illness progressed, all the demons, which they had pacified before in the creative space between them, started flying around and occupying each of them in turn and making them drift apart. He became nostalgic for his background, asking for family members she had never heard of. Before the illness took hold of him even more, and after he deliberately delayed the second bout of chemo that would more than certainly produce the visible results of losing his hair and giving him that hard to miss cancer face, he set off for Kerala, where the remaining members of his family had gathered. An invitation was not extended to her, she did not fail to notice, although it must have been to Alaina, who discreetly broached to her that she was going to join Daddy for a week. Her exclusion stung like a wasp. It was a fast downward spiral from there onwards, both of their relationship and his body, she stretched, talking in a low voice, her eyes looking at the void this time. All her ways of showing off, making him jealous and then returning to his lap, were now reversed.

'I started going out a lot. With girlfriends to start with. But then, I took to the bars alone. After all went quiet in our house and the lights were off I would set off. Alaina was still living with us, and she was not a party girl, even in her early twenties. I got dressed, put heavy make-up on and got out with a pack of cigarettes in my pocket. Ironically, he had stopped smoking by then, and I never understood why. It was too late anyway. Was it another of his tactics to hurt me?'

Her voice is getting hoarser and hoarser and I am astounded to hear what I already know she's going to say.

'I slept with many. Lost count after a while. A true London demographic, in a true Islington pub with extended hours where people from all walks of life could be met. It had the effect I needed it to. It made me numb and, also, it reminded me that I was still alive and a woman and desirable.'

'Alice,' I whisper, 'you have said a lot.'

The pain is palpable in the room, and all I want now is to envelop and protect her from any more that would prove unbearable for both of us and especially for her in the long hours after the session.

'He died in my lap at least, if that's any consolation at all. It was a night when his suffering was beyond belief. He turned down the morphine. He asked me to hold him. "I love you, Alice", he murmured, when drifting into what I thought was another night's sleep. I had never held him on the crease of my arm throughout the night like that, like a baby, before. It was usually me lying on him. In the morning, he was gone.'

The clock ticks 3.51 and I struggle to find words to bring this to an end. Alice has put the cigarette back in her purse. She is still, quiet and calm, as though we have been sitting together on these chairs at an angle for many, many years.

No words

> Loss is one of the most universal experiences and an inevitable part of being human. Yet, the residual long-term melancholy linked with having incurred a significant loss may be a feeling that we are tempted to dissociate from. Here, we meet Nicholas again from Part I, now a young adult in therapy. When Nicholas was twelve his father died unexpectedly from a heart attack. There is a parallel here between the therapist's and the patient's losses and having to mourn for the possibility of a different life, one marked more by the presence of loved ones rather than by their absence. The story is also about the unspoken, and how it is possible to connect with each other's energy and unarticulated states of mind. In traditional psychoanalysis, such tuning into the patient's mind has been called countertransference, but within a relational framework, it is possible to conceive of this space in between two people in a more intersubjective and existential way.

When Nicholas started lying on the couch, the atmosphere and colours in the room and the energy between us changed significantly. Before, there was much empty talk, despite my efforts to help him focus on what mattered, his feelings. Now, there was hardly any talk at all. It would go something like this: he comes in, eyes not focused, preoccupied. Then, he takes his coat off and he swiftly lies down, the soles of his shoes discreetly placed off the couch. He then clears his throat, he lies there looking at the ceiling.

I found myself during several sessions following his gaze, counting the spotlights, one, two, three, four, five. Then, the cracks, three tiny hair-like ones, one more alarming, deeper. Only a year since I last decorated the room.

Nicholas clears his throat again. His breathing speeds as though he was coming round from general anaesthesia. Then, I wait for something more, but a minute later I find myself focusing on the books stuck neatly on the shelves in the bookcase just across the couch. How many on each shelf?

On that late afternoon, pitch dark already before Nicholas had arrived, my eyes fell on Kristeva's *Black Sun* and they could not move on. It was now my turn to clear my throat. I said: 'I was wondering what it felt like to be the son of your father?'

He took a while. Breathing even, eyes still on the ceiling. It was just his thumbs at the top of his interlocked hands that took a life of their own, rubbing circularly against each other. Just as I thought my strange question would fall by the wayside, he said quietly:

'To be my father's son was the only way I knew how to be a son, I guess.'

'Can you elaborate?'

'He was my father, doing fatherly things with me. Taking me to the park, teaching me how to ride a bike, getting me to help him when he did gardening in the summer, even teaching me how to drive the car, even though I was only twelve at the time.'

'At the time?'

'At the time of his death I mean. I guess, I was not his son after that.'

Then he stopped and quiet fell again in the room after that, but something had changed. I noticed I had stopped counting. Instead, I could feel a knot in my throat, just the kind of knot we are all familiar with at the times we try to withhold our tears. I imagined asking Nicholas:

And the colour black? What do you associate the colour black with?

My mother, he would say. *She wore black for many years after my father died.*

Hmm, I see. And how did you feel about it?

I did not like it, he would say in his flat, uneventful voice. *It turned me into an orphan so I would try to hide when she visited my school for a parents' evening.*

Nicholas had told me already, in fact he stressed in his first session, that he didn't like being seen as an orphan. He was the black son instead, I thought, the son of his depressed mother. I imagined that if I said to him just that, he would cry quietly, while he lay on the couch looking at the ceiling. I imagined a young teenage Nicholas lying on his narrow single bed at home looking at the ceiling, tears falling like droplets from a faulty tap. I imagined he had spent many night times crying quietly wanting to be the son of his father, a son who is taken out for walks and to his scouting lessons and for an ice cream after. I imagined missing his father was so unbearable that he had started counting the cracks on the ceiling every night before falling asleep instead of feeling his absence.

I thought I would say:

'Not being the son of your father must have been truly unbearable.'

Instead I said:

'Our time is now up.'

***

The following week, Nicholas arrived as always on time. He took his coat off and then he lay on the couch, the soles of his shoes hanging off the edge. His thin black hair was very shiny, I noticed, and it occurred to me for the first time that he was actually a handsome young man.

'I was thinking,' he said, 'after your question the other day, that my father was actually an orphan.'

'Was he?'

'Yes, from birth.'

I looked at the flower arrangement on my small round Moroccan coffee table. Isabel used to buy fresh flowers every week and put them there in a cream enamel watering can. I used to call it *Isabel's therapy touch.* Sometimes I called it *Isabel's transitional object.* I used to tease her about the therapy touch, but I never told her about transitional objects. I just knew she would not have liked it.

'It's infuriating how infantilising you therapists can be', she had said to me once after walking out of a trial session with a therapist she had found herself, as I deliberately refrained from guiding her, hoping that if it was her own initiative, it would work. She had decided not to persevere with it, she didn't need it, she said. She was a grown woman and if she had doubts about motherhood, it was only natural, as it had not been in her repertoire of what to do in life before meeting me. The flowers had stopped a long time ago. They became rarer while her tummy expanded and they stopped all together after our son's birth. *I guess that makes sense*, I had thought at the time. *She was busy being a mother.* It took me a while to fill the gap and begin buying my own.

'Your father was an orphan from birth?' I asked.

'Yes, his mother died while giving birth to him and his father died fighting in the First World War while she was pregnant. He was totally unexpected as his sisters were grown up when he was born. They brought him up, but everyone called him "the orphan" in the village. It was the one thing I remembered my father being bothered about.'

'It sounds like he was worried that you may become an orphan.'

'Yes, he thought that if he died, I would.'

'Even if your mother was around?'

'Well put. My mother was around, that's all it was.'

'You mean not engaged with you?'

'No, she was a rather distant figure. My father got me ready for school and waited for me at home upon my return.'

He stopped in his tracks. He turned on his side facing the wall. The next thing I heard was like a wail from a wounded dog left on the side of the road to die after being knocked over.

'Nicholas?'

The sound continued intermittently. He then asked me for the box of tissues which I passed on to him. He wiped his nose, turned on his back again.

'I just remembered that my father used to prepare sandwiches for me to take to school with me. He was a food inspector and, also, a fit man who wanted to live for as long as possible. Not very lucky there.'

I could hear the bitterness in his voice, thick like a double espresso swallowed down at once with no sugar.

'I guess it was only right he wanted to live long as he chose to bring me into the world, he wanted a child, a son.'

He seemed for once to want to talk a lot, to get it out of his system, and I held my breath.

'So, he would insist that I needed to have a sandwich at school at about midday to keep my blood sugar even. He would just not get it that I wanted to fit in or at least not to stand out. Nobody else took sandwiches or any other food to school. Some kids would buy lunch from the canteen, but my father had said it was shocking how bad the quality of the food the canteen sold was. Especially as it was catering for children. The thing is, I would throw all his sandwiches away before I got back home from school. The day he died, I got back from school and he was not there. A couple of days later, I discovered a decomposing sandwich in my bag. It's like I knew he wasn't going to be at home that afternoon when I returned from school and I forgot to chuck it away.' His voice cracked again.

When I accompanied Nicholas to the door that day I wanted to tell him how sad I thought the story of the uneaten sandwich was. But I was lost for words when he said it, and too cowardly to diverge from our ritual of silently accompanying him to the door later on. I guess I was worried he would take offence at my pity, but in fact, it was myself that I felt mostly sorry for, as despite doing this job for years, I still found loss as unbearable as he did.

***

Although I have been seeing Nicholas for more than two years now, that session in late November, when I spotted *Black Sun* on my shelf, and the one after, when he talked to me about his father being an orphan and about the uneaten sandwich in his bag, contained the most words that I remember ever being exchanged between us. The long melancholic silences that I have come to associate with Nicholas since then are in fact among the most delectable hours in my practice. Since these two relatively talkative sessions though, I have stopped counting the spotlights and the cracks and the stacked books on my bookshelves. Instead, I sit quietly, listening to his even breathing, following his eyes that now seem to wander round the room, little creases between his eyes and on the sides of his mouth indicating the quick succession of his thoughts, the processing of his feelings.

While Nicholas lies on the couch, Isabel's image comes to mind. The passionate week we had on the small isolated island of Ikaria in the east of Greece while September was ripe with fruit. How many figs had we shared then with sticky fingers? How I could hardly do anything without daydreaming about her the week after. And then quickly, the shared life, me tentatively leaving my toothbrush in her bathroom after a delicious night of sleeping in each other's arms, then moving in. And then soon after, 'the accident', she got pregnant. I could see it now, it was far too soon in the relationship. It all moved quickly after that, buying our two-storey three-bedroom Victorian house in the north of Notting Hill, the nice up-and-coming area around a park where wannabe Notting Hillites moved when they decided to grow a family. Isabel was one of them. A wannabe Notting Hillite I mean, not aspiring to grow a family. She had said it then, quietly, just before falling asleep in my arms on a late summer night in her tiny apartment. Perhaps she could have an abortion and things would be like before, she had whispered.

I didn't pay attention, I thought I could save her and make her happy. Had Nicholas ever tried to save his mother from the black void? Did he ever want to make his mother happy?

Indeed, it was not long after I had these thoughts that Nicholas walked into a session announcing quietly:

'I met a girl. In fact, she asked me out. I like her a lot, though she seems a bit troubled.'

It felt like we had gone through the long winter of his mourning for the one parent he did have, the one whose departure had left him an orphan, and we were entering another, more troubled phase. He would now try to cure his black mother, try to get something out of her for himself at last, and he was bound to fail, just like I had done in my endeavours to save Isabel and get her to be the partner I wanted and the mother I never had.

Another chance

> This story is to an extent about the limits of therapy and to an extent about the crucial difference therapy can make, especially when it feels like a person's life is at stake. Much recent psychoanalytic work has focused on working with the borderline personality disorder presentation clinically. This is not always consistent with a psychiatric diagnosis but, more often, it refers to a psychoanalytic understanding of the term. The description of such patients is often negative, as clinically, they test the ability of the therapist to function, and therefore, to be able to help them. What is not as consistently recognised is that BPD is almost always the result of severe trauma in childhood and parental failure to contain the child's feelings. Therapy on the edge of survival for both the therapist and the patient is at the core of the story below.

I

It was around the middle of our family summer holiday when I received Katia's email, although her name did not bring up in my memory much light at all. If I were to associate Katia Gravi with any season, this would have been the autumn, and more specifically, Halloween, one of the darkest periods of the year, but a remarkably mysterious and beautiful time too. In one of the fraught sessions we have had over the years, she told me that she had deliberately changed the ending of her surname in English, from *-ou* to *-i*, which was still grammatically correct, she said, in Greek, but she particularly disliked getting pinned down, especially, she said, by those who were completely ignorant of who she really was, those who loved to put others into boxes and who thought that once they classified somebody, they understood them. It was, of course, understandable that Katia Gravi felt this way, as she was aware she was easily classifiable, especially under the borderline personality disorder diagnosis, which was becoming a huge trend among my colleagues.

I was not exactly a newly qualified therapist when Katia had found her way to my consulting room about nine years ago, but I guess I felt like one. It was a new experience to rely solely on my private practice for my income and my professional identity as well. I still remember like in a slow-motion film how Katia walked in, wearing all black, or something very dark anyway, her luminous green freckled eyes sitting on pale skin, lips visibly cracked and inflamed red as a result of being dead dry, ebony hair waving around her face and sometimes covering most of it. There is I think something particularly beautiful about women who make a point of wearing no make-up at all, and also, those who almost deliberately draw attention to all the imperfections in their face. Certainly Katia Gravi was one such woman. Black circles under her eyes, dry, cracked lips and some traces of acne on the skin around her lower cheeks, all highlighting her bright eyes, her young white teeth, her ironic smile. I guess another way to put it is that women show their vulnerability to men when they start having feelings for them, and equally, men only develop profound feelings for women when they begin to see their vulnerability, and in Katia's case, it was all there in plain sight from the first minute she walked into my consulting room.

I used to feel awkward thinking about our session in terms of a meeting between a man and a woman, but this is what it felt like between us from day one, and pretending it was otherwise misses the point. I guess I never planned to write a case study about her, nor am I keen on the kind of clinical paper that demonstrates the steps in the treatment's progress as though the author holds a map of the patient's pathology and can take the reader through their trajectory from sickness to health. Thankfully, these are quickly becoming rather out of fashion even for those who insist that only the properly trained analysts hold any power to cure. I have to say, though, the fact that it felt right from the beginning like a man met a woman, made me greatly ill at ease. This was not the only reason for which I sustained doubts about whether I should accept Katia Gravi in my private practice. It felt like no matter what I tried, Katia would be the one setting the terms of our work. Yet the one condition I managed to persuade her to consent to was that she needed to come three times a week. Any less than that would be dangerously ineffective for the severity of her distress, I insisted. Of course, later on she played up with that rule as much as she could, provocatively not turning up for sessions in a row. Yet, it was these sessions that Katia Gravi did not attend that she made her presence most painfully felt to me, I have to say. She was fully aware of that, of course, and the fact that she had found a way to insert her sting into me compelled her to repeat this, again and again.

She was aware of my doubts about taking her on, and this, again, highlighted her vulnerability, which was only thinly disguised by her sarcasm and inappropriately timed smiles. Katia was truly like a magician pulling black and white rabbits out of her sleeve just at the moment you least expected it. The thing she was absolutely honest about from the beginning was that therapy was the last thing she had ever wanted to try, but she also knew it was her last resort, as she would probably have died very soon without it.

This is a rather dramatic premise for the beginning of the therapeutic relationship, and one that inevitably raises an alarm. It is rather too much to put on anybody's shoulders the responsibility of keeping somebody else alive. Yet, it raises the stakes on what therapy can do for people as well. What I mean is that for some who find their way to it, it makes the difference between life and death, rather than how it is often portrayed – some kind of self-indulgent, Woody Allenesque navel-gazing. That was the hook for me, or one of them anyway.

The other thing Katia was honest about from the beginning was what she wanted therapy for. She needed somebody to witness her self-destruction, she said, as though if somebody was there to watch her morbid dance she would manage to keep balancing on the thin rope and not fall screaming down into the abyss. Well, witnessing somebody's life was not a unique role for a therapist, but witnessing somebody's chase with death is quite another story.

The black and white rabbits out of her sleeves though were all the little facts and details that made her situation so precarious and my position as her therapist as well.

White rabbit number one

Pulled out of her sleeve in session ten: Katia was only twenty-one years old and not twenty-five as she had stated in the initial consultation form. So clever of her to anticipate that her true age would raise my doubts even more about taking her on!

Black rabbit number two

Katia was in the regular habit of not eating for two or three days in a row. Her record, she said, was a week, a fast which could only be broken by the relaxation induced by a large glass of red wine, she said. On one occasion, when her fast had included water abstinence as well in the middle of a heatwave while she was on holiday in Greece, she had woken up in hospital from a dehydration coma, and I had endured a long phone conversation during my summer break with a Greek psychiatrist, who had alerted me to the high suicide risk of people with Katia's condition (this is when BPD was officially confirmed).

It was after that summer break that I had received the first blow from Katia, one that I was to remember for years to come. It had seemed right after the hospital incident to confront her with the limitations of what therapy could do for her.

'What position do you think it puts me in, to be traced by a psychiatrist in Greece and to be alerted to my patient's deteriorating condition?'

I was evidently furious with her, when in fact, my anger should really be directed towards myself. As I knew all along, I had made myself very vulnerable through accepting her in private practice without enlisting the help of her GP or even asking her to come to an agreement about keeping herself safe while seeing me. It was the idealism of the beginner I was being guided by, wanting to truly accompany somebody in their journey no matter what places it took us both to. But how can one possibly predict what it feels like to be lost in rough seas, no land in sight?

'Listen, Katia, I am aware that I have agreed to witness your distress, but there are limits to everything. There is an "as if" quality to my consent to being a witness. It will only work to the degree that having somebody understand how bad it feels to be you will eventually make you feel better. But, if all you want is to destroy yourself that makes our work redundant. Abstaining from food and water for days on end in a hot country is a suicide attempt!'

I was so taken by my sense of indignation that I failed to notice how distressed she was while in the room with me. She had hardly said anything. Her skin was pale and her eyes luminous, as she rocked back and forward.

'I agree there is no point to this all', she said, looking at me provocatively. A sadistic smile was forming at the tips of her lips. I could see the true joy she felt at winning over, her anger put into action rather than just in words. 'That's it, I am not coming back.'

I could not believe how close to tears I felt straight after her statement, as I knew fully well she was capable of doing what she had just said. My voice cracked and as a result, I was unable to form any therapeutically effective sentence. All I managed to mutter was, 'This is not the way to end long-term therapy, Katia', but I knew fully well that it was *her* way and that I had just received for the first time the full blow of her destructiveness. Two pleading notes after the aborted session only produced a cheque in the post, the covering note signed, 'Thanks for your help, K.'

II

I suppose it must make me sound like a completely incompetent therapist that I allowed this sequence of events to take place twice more, and I was as ineffective in changing it as the first time it took place. The only difference was that every two-yearly cycle of therapy with Katia Gravi produced a few more black and white rabbits.

White rabbit number three: Katia talking about her family and her past

The more I reflect on what went on between Katia and me, the more embarrassed I feel about much I consented to and agreed with, as it felt like I had no other choice than to accept her terms. Katia refused blatantly to talk about her family, her childhood or her past, stating that only the present mattered and what she was doing now, which is what she wanted me there for. She also argued that it was her therapy and not anybody else's, and if I wanted a textbook patient, I should not raise my hopes that she would ever become one. The latter argument was quite convincing as I agreed with her that every therapy is unique and should be the unpredictable outcome of the meeting between two people. Yet, the sense of secrecy around Katia's past was one of the factors that made me ill at ease and I was not reticent in telling her so. I could discern of course, quite a few things about her through how she was in the present, and that was one of the many exciting premises of the encounter with her. If the past is always within the present, do we need to know about it in order to understand it? I could also tell that Katia was highly intelligent, educated and possibly from a privileged background as I could just about detect the slightest hint of a Greek accent in her impeccable spoken English.

White rabbit number three was pulled out of her sleeve early on upon her return to therapy after her yearly break. It was getting dark, even though it was still early in the afternoon, a combination of heavy black clouds and the rapidly shortening days. I was sitting there wondering if I should switch the light on, but my instinct was right that the semi-darkness was enabling something to emerge that would have possibly never been uttered in full light.

'He used to come to my room in the middle of the night', she said. 'The first time it happened I pretended to be asleep, and all the following ones as well. It hurt like hell, you know when an incredible thing is done to your body, a secret place being invaded that you did not even know you had. I was only eight and I had blood in my knickers for days after. The silent professor, solemn academics are highly valued where I come from, and he was utterly solemn and proper at home as well as at work.'

'Who are you talking about?' I said almost breathlessly. 'What are you talking about?'

'He used to come to my room a couple of times a month thereafter, call of nature, I guess. At least, when it was completely silent, which it was for years, we could both pretend it didn't happen. But then, as I approached adolescence, he started talking, and that I found truly unbearable, as it made it difficult to pretend convincingly that I was fully asleep and for him to persuade himself I was too.'

The air had become stifling in the room and the darkness thick. 'Katia, are you saying your father sexually abused you? Was your father a university professor?'

'He started making cheesy comments, vomit-inducing ones quite honestly, like "your boobies are growing fast, they are deliciously virginal". "Your little pussy knows how to receive a man's penis now", and he would get out of breath as well. Even the pitch dark would no longer conceal all the tears that rolled from my eyes, my pillows were soaked, moisture in the wrong place . . .'

'Could you not tell your mother?' I whispered.

'My mother is a well-known poet. Always in her room, always unavailable. I grew up with nannies, the only living presence in our house were the housekeepers.

'When my periods stopped at sixteen, I had done my research already, expecting it to happen, I knew where to go to terminate things, and since then, I got a lock for the door. I enlisted the help of my beloved housekeeper for that, a round, lovely woman, and I made sure I had no periods either for the year to come, a cleansing fast . . .'

I had no session straight after, and to this day, I don't know if it was the right thing to do, but I allowed Katia to sit in the dark with me for quite some time after the official end of her session, asking her sparse questions to establish some basic facts. She had no contact with her family, she said, after she left home for university in London, it is not like they were chasing after her either. She went to Greece every couple of years, nostalgia for the landscape catching up with her, a couple of good friends from school still trying to keep in touch with her. Her family sent her money though, every month. A respectable amount went into her bank account, yet she did her best not to touch it, her library work producing just enough income for her bedsit and her thrifty existence.

Black rabbit number four

Katia had alluded from the beginning, before her latest disclosure, that sexual risk was her main presenting issue, although of course, the periodic anorexia and deep cutting that sometimes had nearly sent her to hospital with bleeding that she could not stop, could not be ignored. She had asked me from the beginning what I knew about BDSM, and I had been vague in my answers, though she had challenged me on that, alluding that she could have chosen to see a specialist in the matter. Katia was, as I understood, very knowledgeable about the BDSM philosophy and the sense of community it produced, yet, she had hinted again, she had chosen to use BDSM unwisely, increasing the stakes and the risk. But as was so often the case with Katia, what she hinted at was not the same as what was revealed in key moments when a rabbit was being pulled out of her sleeve.

It was the session after her disclosure, and I could see as soon as I opened the door, even before she had come into the room that she was literally black and blue.

'What happened?' I said in a shaky voice. 'You clearly need to see a doctor. Have you been to the A & E already?'

She had a smile fixed on her face throughout the session, which sat almost surreal over two black eyes.

'Don't worry, it's all superficial', she insisted. 'It was quite an experience though, at some point I left my body, I think. I must have fainted, as when I came round, we were in different positions, both of them doing different things to different bits of my body.'

'Both of them?' I muttered feeling my stomach turn.

'Yes', she said, smile widening. 'They were the closest I got to the two faces of my father, a silent and a chatty type, one doing things, the other producing the commentary.'

'Fucking hell, Katia! Why on earth do you think I want to hear all this? It's too much, too much!' I got up pacing up and down, unable to be confined in my seat. I had lost it, I knew as well, but couldn't care less at that moment.

'I am pregnant too, you know', she said, staying very still in her chair. 'I've known for some time. I hoped the dungeon session yesterday would sort that out for good, but no luck so far.'

I sat down, defeated. There were no words.

This time she stayed until the end of the session, mostly still with the smile on. 'I am off', she said a couple of minutes before the end of the session.

'You are off?'

'Yes, we've been there before and there is no point in all this, is there? I am off for ever.'

'Don't do this to us, Katia', I said. At least this time round, my defences were down.

'I will', she said, and for the first time her face was angry and dark. 'Don't you see, I have to do all this, because you won't fuck me, you won't love me, you won't save me!'

Her voice, slightly raised at the end, echoed in my mind for all the months to come. This time, I could not switch off or pretend that this was truly the end, and I could not stop myself worrying. It was the first time I noticed the wall of silence being raised between Isabel and me. Why did I feel I could not speak to her about Katia? She had by now become my secret patient I had talked to nobody about, a personal bet. I also knew by now that she was lying of course when she said she wanted me to witness her distress. She needed me to rescue her, to love her, to absolve her from her past. All this put us of course on even more treacherous ground. Yet, despite persistent anxiety, I decided not to contact her GP. I knew she would experience this as a betrayal, and the danger was that she would never come back. I decided to wait month after month, for her return.

III

As always, Katia Gravi acted unexpectedly. When twelve months passed and I started giving up hope that I would ever see her again, trying to brush away the thought that she may not even be alive by now, the long-awaited email came through asking to come and see me.

This time, she looked somewhat different, more smartly dressed, less pale, less dangerously thin, her hair brushed away from her face. I would be pleased to know that she was doing well, she said. She had been offered a research assistant post by the library manager, and after the necessary abortion she did not feel as compelled to take risks. It was a quiet period of contemplation.

I tried not to feel resentful about all the months of agony and worry I went through, the thought crossing my mind that I had become a container for all her bad feelings, and as a result, she could thrive instead.

'I may even be ready for the kind of therapy you do', she said, the familiar ironic smile back on her face. 'The talking therapy, fundamentally not suitable for people in real distress.'

'Do you mean you may be able to have therapy now that you don't need me as much?' I said, the thought of her last utterance before she had aborted the therapy for the second time still vivid in my mind. I had promised myself that if she ever returned I would confront her with what she had said, I would ask her what she meant when she said that she had to get violated by other men because I would not sleep with her. Yet, I passed. One thing though I managed to do differently this time. I said to her firmly that she needed to give me a month's notice in order to terminate therapy. Breaching this agreement would bring about the end of our work for good, I stressed to her. She agreed reluctantly.

This time round Katia Gravi's therapy was somewhat less eventful and closer to what most of us expect from the course of analysis, talking, making links between the past and the present, moments of insight. There were of course, the times of high danger, when her therapy began to seem futile again. Days of starvation that I could see sculpted in her face, a face whose features I had grown accustomed to read fluently for signs of extreme distress by now. A deep cut on her upper arm that had produced an infection that needed intravenous antibiotics for three days in hospital. She made a point of lifting her long sleeves to show me. Katia always wore fully concealing clothes, covering every inch of her body, and I could not avoid noticing my arousal at the sight of her smooth white flesh, even if she only uncovered a small part of the body which most women expose daily in the summer months. I know this may sound banal for a middle-aged male therapist seeing a young woman in therapy, yet, I was convinced, and still am, that it was the intense emotional intimacy that our particular combination produced that had to be eroticised for lack of any other avenue in the adult mind.

Coming to think of it, how many people's faces do we know so well that we can tell, through looking at them, how many hours they slept last night, whether they had one too many fags and whether they have had a nutritious meal or not? After all, I had been sitting in my room with Katia across from me for fifty minutes each time, three times a week for a total of five years now. But it was not only that. It was Katia's face that wanted to make itself open to being read as though to counteract the secrecy and evasiveness of her words, constantly on the lookout for a mother who would at last get to know her intimately.

White rabbit number five

She walked in triumphantly.

'At last, I have some really good news!' she announced. 'I hear my father is dead! My mother sent one of her notes I never reply to.'

She had never before mentioned that she received notes from her mother, but also her triumph over her father's death, even if her father, it had to be admitted, was a real monster, was a tricky premise for her therapy, I thought. How often, anyway, life and death seem to come together. That very morning, my first son had been born after an earlier than anticipated labour and I had cancelled all the rest of my sessions for the week other than this one with Katia. My plan was to let her know I would begin my Easter break half a week earlier, but now I was stuck. I silently went through how to tell Isabel that I would have to do just a few sessions for this week, as I had a patient in crisis. In crisis Katia Gravi was not, her face remaining as calm and clear as ever, her time-keeping for the sessions impeccable for the first time ever. For the first time as well she gave me some sense and flavour of her early childhood. Apparently, she had been quite close to her mother for the first years of her life. Her mother was warm and tactile, Katia said.

'My memory of my mum is of an elegant and fragrant young woman. Silky sand-coloured hair my mother had, I take my colours from the dead monster, unfortunately. She was truly flowery like a Sarah Kay model, a woman born to be a poet. It is like once I grew taller and wider, once I would not fit into her lap, there was no place for me in her at all.'

'Maybe this is why you have to remain slight, Katia', I murmured. 'In order to fit in somebody's lap.' I had said this unwittingly, but as an afterthought, I wondered whether there was some unintentional innuendo in my utterance, Katia Gravi fitting in my lap . . .

Black rabbit number six

'I had a dream about you', Katia said straight after my two-week paternity break, not that she knew this was the reason I was taking a break of course.

Dreams were one of the seductive features of Katia's therapy. She did not often bring one, but those that she did were very much like her, intelligent, revealing and concealing complex, fragile structures. I was surprised to feel her gaze fixated on me, almost burning.

'You will not like it', she whispered, and I could almost feel the sadistic pleasure in her voice.

Of course, it was never that easy to extract things from Katia, and this was not the first time that she withheld important information from me until nearly the end of the session.

'If you want me to tell you that dream, you had better produce some darkness in this room', she said in an irritable voice forty minutes into the session.

I knew exactly what she meant. The warm and expansive April sun had almost descended onto her face in this mid-afternoon session. I got up and decisively pulled all the shutters closed, leaving just about enough opening in them to see my way back to my chair. I sank quietly back into my chair.

'Well, we were in bed together. It was a comfy couch in your consulting room, but not this one. It is like you had an adjoining room to this, and in that room, there was a couch, and a chair beside it. We were cuddling up, no more than that, and you said you missed me and you were glad I was back. You were caressing my hair which was actually sand blonde and wavy. And then, next thing I know this man walks in with no face, I mean his face was covered by shadows and I could not see it. You went and sat on your chair beside the couch to make space for him and you picked a book and you seemed to be reading and he asked me to go on all fours and lift my dress, it is like I was wearing a nightie. And then, I could see I was heavily pregnant and I knew it was a baby boy. It was your baby, you know.' At this point, her voice cracked and she began to weep silently like a little girl.

I was stunned. Not so much because of the dream you see, but to witness her crying. The thing is, one of the most striking facts about Katia was that she had never before shed a tear in the five years I had been seeing her on and off.

'Katia!' I whispered and I was grateful for the darkness in which I could allow my facial muscles to relax and my eyes to moisten. It is hard to envisage what degree of suffering some people go through, unless someone sat in my chair for a number of years and was open enough in order not to raise walls of defences between this chair and the one across from me.

'I think about the lost babies every day, you know', she said in a weepy voice. 'It doesn't matter who the father was. They are still my babies that I killed.'

'You protected them from a life of suffering, Katia. They would have had too many conflicts.'

'But this was your baby, in the dream I mean, and then, the man without a face started, you know, penetrating me from behind, and I could feel my belly tightening, excruciating labour pain I think it was, and I knew that even though you were pretending to read a book you were watching us. I was trying to understand if you were relieved you had got rid of me or if you got, you know, if you got a kick out of watching me get penetrated by the man with the shadowy face.'

'Katia,' I said being mindful of the time and how I needed to proceed quickly, 'this is a very important dream. In the dream, I am like your mother. I am watching you getting abused, but I am either unable or unwilling to intervene.'

'Or getting your kicks out of it', she said provocatively, her familiar mask-like smile having quickly, I sensed, returned to her face.

'Well, this is your fear, but the important thing in the dream is that I need to withdraw and my withdrawal causes your abuse, exactly like with your mother.'

'Bollocks!' she shouted. I was taken aback. Despite the degree of difficulty of being in the room with her, she had never before raised her voice or sworn at me,

'You are talking bollocks! Yes, be like my mother if it suits you! I told you in the first part of the dream I was in bed cuddling up with you, and then, I was pregnant with your child. A baby boy. Do you have a baby boy?'

Even in the dark, I felt her gaze piercing through me as I sat there speechless.

'Anyway, I'd better be going. It is time isn't it', she said, just as I was wondering how to broach the end of the session. And at exactly 3.50 she walked out of my door.

I received a note from her in the morning of the next session I was due to see her. It read:

'I am not able to carry on. I am sorry for breaking my promise.' It included payment for all the sessions of the current week which was the last one in the month, and I wondered if this was her way of dismissively half-honouring our agreement.

IV

Guilt is one of the most useless, debilitating feelings you can possibly have, but I would have been either insensitive or incompetent or both, had I not felt guilty for my failure to address Katia's erotic transference. And even more shamefully, the guilt stemmed from wondering why I had failed to acknowledge her feelings towards me. Was I too implicated perhaps? And yet, I knew through her dream that what she made of my evasiveness was that I was either too preoccupied or too perverse or both to take proper care of her.

Given all this, it would have perhaps been the safest and neatest thing to do to keep to my promise of never seeing Katia Gravi again. Yet, you may have already guessed that nothing in my management of Katia's case has been neat at all. So, when her email came through in the middle of our family summer holiday, I took a couple of days to get back to her. When her second email came through pleading with me to respond, I had already made up my mind that I would see her again. After all, leaving things unresolved for ever was not good for either party concerned. Guilt extended more than one way of course, as by the time Katia's email reached me in the midst of our two-week holiday in a family resort in Minorca, it had become clear to me that my relationship with Isabel had been mortally afflicted by the most dangerous disease of long-term coupledom, emotional alienation. I could not help but wonder if Katia's email provided thirst-quenching excitement in what would have been otherwise a painfully tiring and relentless family vacation with a restless toddler.

This time, I was determined to avoid any clinical errors to the degree that I could trust myself at this point. So, as soon as Katia walked in my consulting room in early September, I rushed to acknowledge that my therapeutic credibility was at stake, as I had stated I would never see her again if she ended the therapy in the way she did. I added that I thought it was important to try and resolve things. I don't know if it was my impression or hope, but Katia seemed somewhat softer, less dark from the moment she walked in. Although of course, there was a hint of irony in her smile as a response to my statement, it was also followed by politeness. She was grateful I consented to see her again, she said.

Then, I proceeded to address error number two and state that I was aware that I had failed to address her erotic feelings towards me and she was right to reprimand me for that before she aborted her therapy for the third time.

She leaned forward, as though she intended to pat me on the shoulder like a mother about to reassure an overanxious child. 'Jake', she said, and it was the first time in six years that she uttered my name, with confidence and ordinary simplicity as well. 'You were right of course. You stood for my mother in that dream, the only love of my life, even if shortly. But now, I have had a second chance. I am in love. Her name is Natasha', she added with a wry smile. 'She is as beautiful and fragrant as my mother was in these early years.' She then proceeded to give me her first promise ever, that she would never leave me again, she would never leave therapy before it came to its natural end. She needed to work on making herself better, she said, as life seemed worth living for the first time ever.

I can't pretend that I did not feel an attack of the green-eyed monster of jealousy in that session and many repeated visits in the sessions after, but there was relief there too, as I could see that at last Katia had begun to acknowledge love when it came her way. Letting someone else get close to her would prevent her from falling into the abyss any more. That meant that our relationship could be more affectionate too. And to this day, I continue to see Katia Gravi regularly, having reduced her weekly sessions gradually from three to two to one, like a parent waiting patiently for their offspring to sail off for good, despite the sad knot in their throat at the knowledge that being abandoned will have to be the end result.

The scar

> This story is about transgression and the permanent scars it leaves behind. Though in the story the form transgression takes is around breaking the ultimate taboo of the therapeutic encounter, and proceeding to have sexual contact with a patient, transgression, more often than not, takes many subtler forms. In a relational context, both therapist and patient benefit enormously and can take pleasure from the therapeutic encounter, yet, the ethical premise of therapy is that, at the same time, the therapist makes the space for the patient's unresolved feelings and entanglements, and in this sense, the relationship is not an equal one. Any agenda on the part of the therapist, other than making the space for the patient, constitutes a potential transgression. So, at the core of psychotherapy is a paradox; The therapist is an actively involved party in the intense and intimate relationship that therapy is, and yet, he/she needs to abstain from using the patient for the satisfaction of his/her own needs.

This was the one thing, she said, that she could never forgive Dr Strauss for, that she could not meet somebody new without having to tell the story of how she got the scar. I still remember vividly the first and only session that Fenia missed, as it was the morning Isabel announced, over a quick coffee before leaving for work, that she wanted out. That our relationship was over. When I sat quietly in my consulting room, to enjoy the second coffee of the day during the time that would have been Fenia's late morning session, I reflected on what she often said, how scars stay with us for life, and also, how they always have a story to tell.

It was hard to know what I thought of Fenia, a lively and vibrant woman who had entered my consulting room six months ago. I oscillated from warm feelings that sometimes, rather sadly, I found alarming, to disbelief, thankfully not lasting for long, to dismay about my foolishness that I had taken her on at all. You see, a woman sleeping with her ex-therapist, then going to see another male therapist straight after the event, was not exactly promising ground for a positive therapeutic outcome.

Nowadays, it almost sounds like a fairy tale to hear that a therapist is having sex with his female patients, or at least with one of them. It is committing professional suicide. A complaint, and then being struck off are almost certain following such a transgression, as crossing this one boundary is the ultimate taboo of the therapeutic encounter. Yet, except in my brief moments of disbelief, I did not doubt Fenia's story, or that things could turn out so darkly for somebody appearing to be normal and almost, I would say, psychologically healthy.

Fenia was in her early forties. Attractive, despite not looking like a twenty-five-year-old like many of the forty-somethings in the West London suburbs she lived in. I mean despite her clear middle-class demeanour, she was not platinum-blonde, she was not wearing UGG boots and skinny jeans, and one could even still see the effect of two pregnancies in the discreet trace of a bump and the slight greying of her dark-blonde hair. She was creatively, but not impeccably dressed, and sometimes, I had noticed her coat had been cross-buttoned, as she must have left home in a hurry to come to our session. Fenia was always in a hurry, juggling a very successful consultancy business she ran from the front room of her Victorian house and being there for her two still relatively young children.

She was grateful to me to have taken her on, but she had also been suspicious of me. Was she really to blame for that? On my best days, I could just about believe that if we could swing together in this dance between suspicion and hope, maybe, just maybe, she would be better for it and I would be proud of myself to have taken the risk.

Dr Strauss was in his early sixties when Fenia went to see him five years ago. She must have been in her late thirties, her children still very young, the youngest just about a toddler. Her father had just died tragically of chronic obstructive pulmonary disease, a heavy smoker throughout his life. As much as Fenia was glad that she had been there just before he died to hold his hand and say her goodbyes, she had also resented him for once again taking centre stage in her life, when she had two very young children to look after. Her father, she told me, was a Peter Pan character, the eternal child, never quite an adult, always doing his thing, whether seeing other women as her mother suspected or travelling to faraway places on a whim and spending all the family's money. And yet, somehow he managed to be adored by her mother and her older sister and her as well of course. He could get away with anything, Fenia said, but she could just not forgive him for dying on her from a self-inflicted illness shortly after her daughter was born and robbing her of all the warm, loving attention she had always known she would be able to give to her first daughter.

She liked Mr Strauss, and he immediately became a warm and affectionate father figure for her, the caring father she always craved. An attentive listener, she said, at the beginning, it felt like he was holding his breath for her. It happened very quickly, her falling hard and fast for him, I mean. Again, the erotic transference is almost such a cliché that one does not quite believe in it. Yet, in Fenia's case, walking into Dr Strauss's office, literally days after her father's death, it was almost as predictable that she would develop erotic feelings for him, especially for the kind of therapist that he was, warm and attentive as she described him, as hydrogen and oxygen combined in a chemistry lab is likely to produce water.

Fenia had never had therapy before, but once she made a decision, she was very quick to act, you see; she just was one of those women, happy to follow her gut feeling. And this was precisely what was the hard thing for Fenia now, that she followed her gut feeling and she was wrong, that and the scar of course. What I found sad, I had to say, though I had never told her, was how all this had affected her relationship with her husband, a husband chosen to be the exact opposite of her father, mature, reliable, putting her first. Yet Fenia never quite forgave him for not being like that first man she so adored.

'I was considering a divorce well before anything close to an affair had started happening, you know', she said in one of our first sessions.

'Were you?'

'Well, yes. If I could fall so madly, so easily for somebody else, surely this was a sign that our relationship was over, don't you think?'

'No, because this somebody else was your therapist. You see?'

'You mean that it was not real because he was my therapist? It was a transference? I still don't get this jargon, I have to say. . . . In any case, Dr Strauss (funny to still call him that after what happened between us, I still cannot get to call him by his name) . . . Dr Strauss never talked about transference. It was clear that he considered from the beginning all feelings between us real.'

'You mean when you told him about your feelings for him, he considered them real?'

'. . . But I didn't tell him for a very long time, for years, and then, he told me, in fact . . . then, it all happened.'

'Could you not tell him?'

'No. I was so intimidated, shy, like a twelve-year-old. Ridiculous!'

'Fenia, what do you mean "he told you, and then it all happened"? Can you explain?'

That scene of how they first got together had been replayed in our sessions several times, like pressing the rewind button again and again. She had some memory lapses about how things developed so quickly, and as much as I told her several times that the fact that an intelligent, perceptive woman like her could not clearly remember the sequence of events of something so important that happened, after all, not that long ago, indicated trauma, she still blamed herself for it. It is sad and striking at the same time to notice how much abuse and trauma operate similarly in both children and adults, turning their hatred inwards against themselves like a self-devouring monster.

It was one ordinary session, as far as she was concerned, though she had been aware for some time, for months, possibly for a year or more, that her erotic feelings were being reciprocated. The signs were clear and many and hard to miss. During that same time, Fenia had started experiencing intense anxiety and panic attacks, though she could not put two and two together – how her panic and fear of dying or going mad were an expression of the knowledge that things were no longer safe with Dr Strauss, that she was into an incestuous re-enactment. For that session, she had chosen to wear her long, straight black dress, a dress she had since she was twenty and that she had also chosen to wear at her father's funeral. Geoff was away travelling for work, and Fenia began the session saying how she had noticed that she always experienced palpitations and panic when he was away. She didn't get it, she said, as she was really not that close to him any more. Dr Strauss leant back on his chair, eyes closed, arms crossed against his chest. This was a snippet of a memory that Fenia would revisit for several sessions. It was an unusual posture to take, she had never seen him close his eyes like that before. He struck her as vulnerable, almost frail.

'I think your anxiety about your husband being away is to do with your feelings for me', he said slowly after a while, his voice wavering. 'Your feelings for me are a threat to your relationship with Geoff.'

'Yes', Fenia whispered, feeling stunned. She never thought that this moment would ever come.

In the replay of the scene, I asked her several times how old she was emotionally, when she said that 'yes', as she always struck me like a very young girl. Eventually, she remembered her father, taking her to the cinema when she was six. They watched *Kramer vs. Kramer*. She still remembered his hand heavy on her eyes during the few sex scenes, though she could still watch them between his fingers. She had figured out then, that this was a special visit that she had been chosen for. She secretly thought she must have been her father's favourite, if he chose to go out to the cinema with her, when he was considering a divorce from her mother. He cried during the film and held her hand, and this was the only time she clearly remembered seeing her father looking so frail other than when he became ill later on of course.

The rest was all a blur. How Dr Strauss moved to the sofa next to her, holding her hand and tousling her hair for what felt like a long time. I suggested she was still six at that point, but then it all moved very fast and it was sex, penetration, and then, over. She remembered clearly his frailty afterwards though, her agony about whether it was guilt or a heart condition that got him out of breath, and if she would end up being the cause of his death. Then, it was the talk and that was in a way the most traumatic bit of all. It could no longer be therapy of course, now that this had happened, he said. He could still meet her regularly here, he could meet once a month, and then, it was up to them what they wanted to do, they would both have an equal say on that. He still kept the time frame and finished the session promptly at 12.05 pm.

Suspended was how Fenia felt afterwards. During both day and night it felt as if she lived in a dream, the scenes replaying in her mind like broken footage. And yet, the sex scene utterly escaped her, what she felt during their contact, and if there was any pleasure at all in it that she had experienced. There was definitely no climax, she knew that much.

One night, exactly one month before Fenia came to see me, she woke up like many nights before around 4 am, the scenes from their last encounter flashing through her mind. She would have been due to see Dr Strauss for therapy the following morning, were it not that their last encounter had meant the end of their regular sessions. As she lay there, unable to go back to sleep, she was driven to palpate her breast. It was almost as though an external force, she said, guided her hand to her breast, and there, just above the nipple of her right breast, there was a small, hard and distinct lump.

'So what did you do when you found it? What did it feel like?'

'I went over it again and again, every time expecting that the next time it would not be there, that I had imagined it, and every single time it was exactly on the same spot, a hard pea, just beneath my skin. Then, I could not help it. I switched the table lamp on and I woke Geoff up. I guided his hand on my breast and I could just see in his eyes the same terror that had spread through my body like a heatwave.'

I still remember what it felt like when she told me this, a cold hand squeezing my throat, strangling me. It was just not fair, I thought, too much, far too much for one person to bear.

'We made love that night and it was ecstatic, our bodies melting together. Why could I not see he loved me for all this time? I noticed though, that he avoided my breast, not in a disgusted way at all, more as if he was too scared of this little pea and how big it could prove to be, how it could choke our lives together to death.'

The rest was history. Geoff insisted that Fenia had a private consultation, they had health insurance through his work. The following morning she had a biopsy and three days later a diagnosis of a grade I invasive carcinoma. Her wide lumpectomy excision was scheduled for two days after that. But here was the catch: the post-operation biopsy could detect no cancerous cells in the small excised lump. It appeared to be benign. And to this day, Fenia does not know if there was a mix-up in the first biopsy results or if, as the surgeon tried to convince her, clearly dreading a potential lawsuit, all cancer cells had been removed with the first biopsy and there were none left by the time of the operation.

As for Dr Strauss, Fenia informed him about her condition, hoping that his distress, concern and care about her would be palpable, that he would ask to meet her straight away. He did sound worried and somewhat distraught, yet, he reminded her that they could no longer meet for therapy now, and that he would see her as prearranged in a few weeks' time. Before Fenia hung up after their short phone conversation, he added, 'Would you let me know you are well after the operation though?' and the more than ordinary kindness in his request left Fenia with the impression of a gentle and somewhat frail man. This was the best part of him that she was left with, she said.

By the time Fenia walked into my consulting room, she had written to Dr Strauss to inform him she would not be meeting him again and she had also told Geoff all that had gone on. They cried together and held hands. She knew then that they would be all right. Yet, to this day, the one thing she could not get over was the scar the operation had left her with. It was not that she was bothered at all about the aesthetics of it, she said. Every time she took her daughter for a swim in the pool at their local health centre, she could see her eyes fixating on it. 'The pink scratch on your booby', her daughter called it endearingly, and that's all it looked like.

Yet, every time Fenia projected herself onto her unknown future, she wanted to assert her freedom to meet another man, and not to have to retell her story.

    I, for my part, cannot always see why it is so hard to accept a scar. I told her many times that life for all of us is like a collection of scars, and one should be proud for remaining whole despite them. Yet, every single time I said that to her, Fenia gave me one of her sceptical smiles. In our last session two days ago, she said, 'Yes, but my scar is real.'

Love actually

> The need for a maternal container when this has failed in one's childhood can be overwhelming. Yet, looking for a containing mother in one's relationships, and even in one's therapy, can be unrealistic, especially when the phantasy is that unconditional love and being rescued can be achieved in a pure form. In this short story, we meet Bella, from Part I, who was given the role of containing her mother's distress during the turbulent time of her parents' separation. Rescuing a patient, may be a temptation for the therapist as well, but it invariably conceals a wish to rescue oneself. Yet, to provide containment through respectful listening and being there may be the ultimate aim of therapy, and also what makes a real difference.

The month after Isabel moved out was dark, as expected. Work seemed to be the only refuge, as even spending time with Jackson, something which usually filled me with joy, reminded me painfully of what could have been.

The one area in my life that seemed to work well was my practice, which, now that I had settled on twenty-five hours a week, I considered complete. It gave me a satisfying income and enough time to pick Jackson up from nursery every afternoon as well as enough room to develop as a therapist, to engage and think. When Isabel had announced her leaving, I felt compelled to offer her the house, despite my fear that it would compromise my practice hugely. I would have to find somewhere to rent, somewhere to practise from as well, my income would go down drastically. I was instantly reminded of how vulnerable being a self-employed therapist made me. I relied on a family house, on a stable, long-term relationship. I had been foolish. None of these things were to be relied on. I should have known better. Thankfully, Isabel and I worked as a team much better during the separation than we had ever done as a couple. She wanted to go back to her apartment in Notting Hill, she said, she would lose the rent, but as long as I was happy to pay the nursery fees etc. she was fine with that. She would turn the small guest room into a nice room for Jackson, where he could stay during the three nights a week when I worked late evenings in my practice.

The agreement fell into place easily, and with less than an hour's discussion. I would still pick Jackson up every afternoon, and then, Isabel would take over from five o'clock three evenings a week, when I worked late, and she would drop him off in the morning as well. Weekends would be shared, but Jackson would stay with me for four nights a week to preserve continuity with what he still considered to be his home. What was not acknowledged in this easy agreement, I had thought afterwards, was that I would shoulder the lion's share of Jackson's care, including all the household duties that would now fall solely on me, but I guess implicit in this was Isabel's statement of independence, a reminder of her bitterness about being lured into motherhood without feeling she had given her full consent. The other implicit realisation in all this was how easy it seemed to no longer be a couple, a family, how easy it seemed to be for her to give up on our life together, like the latest trendy garment that she no longer needed as part of her ever evolving wardrobe.

On the Tuesday afternoon when I found Bella Smith's message on my answerphone, just before setting off to pick Jackson up, the feeling of emptiness that had settled in my stomach was hard to disguise. None of the sessions I had this morning was bad, but none was terribly exciting either. It had felt like I was going through the motions, perhaps the worst possible feeling in terms of justifying a full fee. I tried to remind myself that constancy and reliability and benign listening were what most of my patients were happy to pay for, rather than the sharpness of my interventions. I surprised myself by calling Bella back and offering her an appointment on the spot. It had helped that she had let me know in the message that her schedule was flexible, but had I not decided I was full for now?

The first thing that struck me when I met Bella a week later was her looks. She had the kind of face that I immediately found attractive in women. A face that changed instantly from extraordinarily beautiful to unkempt and even ugly, according to the mood that was painted on it; how her mood coloured the light falling on her features and how it made its angles sharp or honed. I could call this rare phenomenon an authentic face, I thought quietly. It helped that today was a typical April day with clouds covering the sun one minute then brightness falling on Bella's face the next, and a quick shower taking all the light away and leaving both of us in the semi-dark.

Did I accept patients with the diagnosis of borderline personality diagnosis, Bella had asked me, sending me a sideways look and a quirky, young-girl smile. She was given the diagnosis in her early twenties while receiving intensive treatment in a prestigious inpatient psychoanalytic establishment, one of the last remaining in the country funded by the NHS. She was now in her late thirties and she felt her troubles were much more ordinary, yet once she'd been diagnosed with a disorder of the personality, it felt like the stigma stayed for life.

'In my experience, it is often the person's family that should actually receive the diagnosis rather than the patient themselves.' I surprised myself with how quickly I had bypassed neutrality in one of my first interventions, but it had seemed like an instant way to win Bella's appreciation, as she sent me one of her luminous smiles.

'Would you like to tell me what had happened and why you needed such intensive treatment?' I rushed to continue with more traditional assessment tasks such as history taking.

'Oh, I was a real mess back then. It was the penultimate year of my degree in English literature at Oxford. It is not uncommon, in fact, for Oxbridge students to go loony, especially those of us who were there with a scholarship and expected to excel. It seemed like the better I did, the more mental I went until it all collapsed.'

'Did you fail your degree?'

'No, surprisingly, I still managed to finish with distinction, but my mother had to shoulder all the funding for the last year.'

'So, what were the symptoms that led to hospitalisation?'

'Ooh!' she hesitated. 'But I am nothing like that now.'

I leaned forward in full therapist's mode now. 'Bella, I am not going to reject you because your symptoms were severe. I know already that they must have been very severe in order to be given access to the only intensive psychoanalytic inpatient service in the country.' I surprised myself even further upon realising that I had decided already to take her on before hearing any of her story.

'Back then, I was starving myself to death. I was using sleeping pills throughout the day that I had stolen from my mother's bathroom cabinet. I was cutting every day as well.' She said all this quickly, with a smile on her face, the kind of smile that produced sharp angles. I could see suddenly that physically she was somebody who had been through a lot.

'Surprisingly, I was closer to death when I was finally admitted than those who take overdoses and attempt suicide, something that you may want to know I never did.'

I closed my eyes slightly, allowing the quick variations of light to flicker in front of my vision. What was it about Bella that brought on all these feelings within the first ten minutes of the session? A little girl-like intense vulnerability; I wished to protect her, to reassure her, to tell her that it would all be all right now that she had found me. I was reminded, not without shock, that this was how it had all started with Isabel. Did that mean that I should not take her on after all? Surely, having a sense of these feelings from early on was protective, for both of us.

'... It was daily group work and daily analysis I had there. I hated the group, I remained completely silent for the first six months, but retrospectively, it proved to be a better experience. You gain so much from hearing about others' stories and struggles.'

Shit, I seem to have lost a good chunk of what she was saying. Lost in translation ...

'Was there something in particular about the individual analysis experience that was difficult?' I asked, trying to gain ground again.

'I guess you can call it a case of negative transference', she smiled wryly again. 'Sorry, but I have been acquainted with the jargon since. Everything seemed to be down to my aggressive urges, my wish to destroy, my envy of the good breast and of my own goodness. In the end, I was using her own language to mock her. I tell you, she didn't like that at all!'

Here was, I thought, another shade in her features, sarcasm painting her face sharp, while her eyes stayed playful. It struck me that she didn't seem worried that she was mocking another therapist in her first session with me.

'I knew straight away that you are not the kind of therapist that she was, which is why I can speak freely about her', she added, as though reading my thoughts. 'Anyway, there was some positive that came out of the experience, I no longer had to be the good girl. I could indeed express all my aggression and hatred freely.'

'Did you feel you had to be the good girl somewhere else before?'

'I guess!'

There was silence for a few minutes in which I wondered if she was mocking me as well. Even if she was, the feeling of deep connection had been established too firmly to be shaken now. When this happened, it made everything worthwhile in the work, and in my experience, it was as instant as an electrical circuit between two live wires.

'Look, I don't want to appear defensive, but this period of my life seems very far away now. I am in my late thirties and I haven't even remotely tried to be a good girl for a very long time. But yes, in my teens, my mother was all over the place when she was going through a divorce with my dad. It was not even a choice; I had to be her carer, her supporter, to be the good girl.'

She seemed angry and exasperated, close to tears. It occurred to me that this was the first genuine emotion that she had expressed directly since she had walked in. Was I feeling all her feelings instead of her, her pain, her vulnerability, the hurt of not being seen? Was this what I did with Isabel, take all her feelings on and try to sort them out for her, was this what had made it all go wrong?

'Yes, but it all sounds like this was not acknowledged or worked through in therapy. If your therapist focused on your aggression and self-destructiveness, she did not quite see that taking it all out on yourself was all the power you had under the circumstances.'

She looked at me as though seeing me for the first time.

'Correct', she said dryly.

The weather had now settled into dark grey cloud and rain poured down outside the bay window. It did not feel much like April after all. I asked her if she would like the floor lamp switched on and she said no, remarking that she preferred the dark, a comment that I was almost expecting. I was aware of the time and how more than half of the session was gone, and that I had not yet got the full picture.

'I was wondering what brings you here now?' I said, aware of the discrepancy between the formality of my tone and the warmth of my feelings.

'Well, this is what I thought I would be talking about, but instead you took me down different paths.'

Was she flirting with me? A thought flashed through.

'As I said earlier, I am nothing like before. After I finished my degree, I got a job as a junior editor in a publishing house. The money was crap, but it was a sought-after job for most of our lot, as you end up doing for work what you have studied and love, reading literature. Work helped a lot to stabilise things, and this is what I am still doing on a more senior level. The good thing is that I am also freelance now, which means that I can work from anywhere I like, though this has proven somewhat more challenging psychologically.'

'Because of the lack of routine?'

'Yes, I guess. I have too much time on my hands, which reminds me of those years of being a student again.'

'And?'

'The main problem, I guess, is relationships. It has always been. I pick up the wrong guy, almost deliberately. I can see how it is going to fail right from the beginning and I delude myself that as I can see it coming all along, it won't hurt when it happens, and yet, when it all falls apart, it hurts just as badly nevertheless.'

I nodded. This made sense. It also sounded strangely familiar.

'The last one hurt more than I expected. What was different was that he was a writer, a published one, which is a big thing in my area of work, as you may know. So, there was an obvious connection right from the start, and though I could see his inconsistencies, how he would shower me with love and then disappear for days, all in the name of artistic expression and creativity, I was still too naive to see the obvious, that he was of course cheating.'

'I am sorry to hear that', I mumbled, being aware at the same time that Bella had completely bypassed the area of her sexuality, coming close to it for the first time when implying she had fallen in love with the wrong guy. I thought I would take the risk.

'Were you in love with him?'

She laughed sarcastically and the sharp angles came through again.

'I thought you therapists had more sophisticated language for these things. Look, it is always a crush that invariably ends up in disaster. That's what it always is. The problem I have that has brought me here is that I can only eat when I am in a relationship. And right now, as I also spend days in a row not meeting another soul, this has become rather dangerous.'

I took a discreet look at her. As a male therapist, still relatively young, I had unwittingly trained myself never to focus my gaze on a female patient's body, to give my attention in other ways. I knew from the beginning that something did not add up in Bella's appearance and I could see what I had missed quite clearly before my eyes now. Behind the baggy track suits and the roomy sweater, what I had assumed to be a lefty intellectual statement, she was completely, utterly emaciated. My heart sank in the same way it did every time I knew that I had reached a therapeutic impasse.

She came back before I had time to speak. 'I know what you'll say, but you need to understand this. I am not an anorexic. I don't care about being thin, though I have never been fat either. I guess food doesn't interest me that much anyway. But right now, I am down to six stones, which I know is dangerous for me. If you can just take me on for three times a week therapy, we can work out a schedule for my eating between us. All I need is somebody to remind me that I need to have three meals a day, to supervise that. Can you help?'

On that note, completely unexpectedly, she burst into tears and the vulnerability that I had sensed from the beginning was there plain to see under the cloudy sky as well as the place she had won in my heart.

***

Bella Smith was the reason I sought help and for this I'll always be grateful to her. I did not want to turn her down as just the thought of it made my chest ache, but the work with her presented me with so many challenges on so many levels. It took a while to know what kind of help I needed, as supervision was too formal a setting, I felt, to honestly explore my feelings, and for whatever reason, I felt a strong aversion to the idea of going back to therapy. As had often happened in my life before, I came across Mrs Grahams's group just at the right time and it proved to be, at least at the beginning of my work with Bella, exactly what I needed. I don't know if I was attracted more to the second part of its name, 'a professional contemplation group', which seemed to define exactly what I was looking for, or, more unwittingly, to the first part of the name, 'on losing and not being lost'. It was good to have that acknowledged, though I did not feel ready in any way yet to begin talking about my losses. I was explicit from the beginning that I wanted to join because of a patient that stirred up many personal feelings but also that losing and being lost resonated with me much at this point in my life. As is always the case in groups, I received the odd antagonistic comment about Bella and my feelings for her being too complicated, but overall the presence of older women in the group, and Mrs Grahams herself, felt soothing and containing. From getting practical advice about referring Bella to her GP for a dietary programme that she would need to follow along with therapy, to understanding better the place she was putting me in, that of a mother, keeping her in mind 24/7, spoon-feeding her. Even my more complex feelings were understood in a helpful way, my need to rescue vulnerable women like my mother, to mother them so that they could be there for me. It occurred to me that in that respect, Bella and I were quite similar as she had also tried and managed to keep her mother in one piece during a turbulent adolescence, to even be there for her little sister, while at the same time taking it all out on herself.

Six months into the therapy, things seemed more settled than I could have hoped for at the beginning. I had explained to Bella in the first session that I was nearly full when I saw her for an assessment and that I had not anticipated a three sessions a week commitment, even if she was flexible with the times. We had agreed that we would keep to it for six months to a year, depending on how things were going and that we would cut down soon after. This little piece of rejection I gave her at the beginning also reassured me about my ability to set boundaries with her. My other condition was that she would see her GP for getting specialist dietary help. In fact, her GP was sufficiently alarmed to refer her straight away to a specialist and to arrange to meet with her regularly to monitor her weight, and as much as Bella mocked the medical system, the reality of her physical condition along with the threat of hospitalisation, acted as a natural boundary of our work as well.

When she came for a session on a sunny October morning, looking much healthier than when I had first seen her, I thought, not without some sadness, that it was time we began reducing the weekly sessions. I was about to begin discussing this with her when she gave me one of her sarcastic smiles, while at the same time, as she often did at the beginning of a session, searching my face to make sure that I was OK and that I would manage to be with her, to survive her tribulations.

'Yesterday,' she said, 'I had the night of my life.'

I hesitated at what seemed an unmistakable sexual innuendo in her voice.

'I met a guy', she continued.

I remained silent, sensing that I was about to be provoked.

'We ended up in my place. It was the best sex I ever had.'

She paused, waiting for a reaction, which I was determined not to give her.

'Won't you ask me something?' she said.

On that, she had the effect she wanted and I felt the first stirring of anger and irritation.

'Bella, in my experience as a therapist, one-night stands are rarely sexually gratifying, so I am waiting to see where this is going.'

'And who said it was a one-night stand? Would you please stop projecting on me?'

I sensed an intense blushing in my face, which made me feel even more embarrassed.

'It was with somebody I have been seeing for a while. It was in fact doing things differently, dating rather than going to bed with somebody who is evidently a loser, just to prove the very fact.'

She paused and stared at me, this time almost with sympathy.

'Look, I am sorry I didn't tell you. I didn't know if it was going anywhere. I didn't want to start obsessing over the guy, just for nothing. In fact, he is the main reason I have been putting on weight so steadily. We have been meeting for dinner most nights. And the other thing is, I told him about my eating struggles, I told him about coming to see you.'

'Oh, so he knows about me, but I don't about him, not until today at least?' I caught myself not managing to conceal the hurt from my voice and I blushed again at the ridiculousness of it all.

'He actually knows all about what you do as well. He is a trainee therapist. Partly, I didn't want to tell you because I felt embarrassed I was using one of these dating sites for the first time ever. So many friends of mine are using them and they all said the same, you have a good chance to find somebody who is a real match.'

'And you knew he was a therapist from his profile?'

'Well, a trainee therapist, but not far from qualifying. He just said he had an interest in psychoanalysis and literature, which I thought was a good match for me. Why are you asking?'

I tried to steady my voice, to gather my thoughts in a way that made sense of the indignation and hurt that I was still feeling. I noticed she was tapping her foot nervously on the little multicoloured rug in front of her chair.

'I just think it is interesting that soon after coming to see me, you actively searched to date somebody involved in the therapy world and on top you chose to keep it a secret from me.'

'Meaning?' she said, the tapping of her foot intensifying at the same time.

'Well, it is almost as though you are looking to find a substitute of me with whom you can have a sexual relationship.'

She stayed silent for a long while. I noticed it was one of the few times that she was not smiling or grimacing in some way. Her eyes looked sad and in the melancholy she exuded she looked more beautiful than ever. I knew it was the wrong interpretation to make at the wrong time. I realised in the silence that, in what I said, I abruptly and inappropriately sexualised our relationship. The thought came chillingly to me that, effectively, she was right, I was projecting. It was me in fact who wanted to be in bed with her rather than the other way round. Sadness came over me slowly as well. Had I ruined for ever the chance of helping somebody I, after all, cared about?

Ten minutes had passed and neither of us made eye contact or spoke. I had to be the one to take the risk.

'Bella, in the silence I have been thinking that I got that wrong. It may have been the other way round. That you got something secure and safe from the therapy relationship with me, which allowed you to take the risk of dating somebody worthwhile for the first time.'

She sighed with relief.

'In the silence,' she said calmly, 'I have been staring at the door. I thought that I am bound not to ever get that right. Intimacy brings about abandonment for me. As soon as I get close to somebody, I have to lose them. I thought I may have to lose you, to walk out.'

'Walk out?'

'Yes, I don't know why, but what you said was truly off.'

'It was, I think,' I nodded, 'because it implied that you didn't truly fancy the guy you are dating, but you fancied me, rather than acknowledge that you needed to use me to find somebody you could feel close to in your real life.'

'Yes, like my mother wanting me to be there for her rather than her supporting me so that I can get out there and get things for myself.'

'Quite!'

'It was the first time, you know, I let a guy give me pleasure. The first time I could let go and let somebody bring me to an orgasm.'

She looked at me in the eye and I could see that it was not provocation that she was confronting me with, but the reality of growing up, of asking me to be there and support her to do just that so that she could begin at long last to get good things for herself.

***

After Bella left, I dialled steadily and calmly Isabel's flat phone number, making sure I dialled 141 first to conceal my number. I knew Isabel would be at work at this time. And indeed, exactly as I was expecting, a bloke picked up the phone, seeming to be perfectly at home in her apartment.

Part IV

Ellie and Jake

> Ellie and Jake meet in a professional development group run by Mrs Grahams. They are strangers to each other, yet, unbeknown to each of them, they have both incurred a parallel loss. They have both been recently abandoned by their long-term partner. Such loss has also brought up, for each of them, previous losses and abandonments from childhood.

On losing and not being lost

> Groups are the arena par excellence for the unfolding of the unconscious. It does not take long for strong feelings to develop between group members, as well as strong projections. It is also not uncommon to become subject to hostility or to be taken over by an inexplicable and irrational force of attraction to another member of the group. The nature of sexual attraction is also paradoxically connected with loss, the desire to lose oneself in another, to heal one's wounds through containment, understanding, connection and no longer having to be separate. In this short story, the focus is on loss, and how it can be the motivating factor in creativity and a sense of a profound connection with another.

When Isabel told him that it was all over, he gave her a hug spontaneously. She stayed in his arms obediently, still, like a little girl. She was not quick to pull back either when he finally let go of her. But she looked at him inquisitively, as though asking, 'Have you understood what I just told you?'

And then, he could not hold in. 'It is not really like you surprised me there, by the way', he said in a cold tone. 'It would take a very thick skin not to pick it up.'

'So, why the hug?' she murmured, as though she had just been slapped.

'It was a goodbye hug', he said firmly and walked off, feeling that, at least temporarily, he could have the upper hand.

Mrs Grahams's group was very quiet today, and although he was not usually one to appreciate silence in groups, thinking that most of the time it was an excuse for the insecure to hide, he had now become accustomed to the contemplation that Mrs Grahams was unique in creating, a sweet glue that bundled the group together. He noticed however, that there were two newcomers in the group today and wondered what they made of the long silence. Mrs Grahams, confident through decades of experience, did not seem to bother about such things, yet he could see that the attractive honey-blonde woman on his right, dressed in a trendy, yet arty way that clearly stated her individuality, was rather nervous sitting in a room with strangers where nobody talked. After all, he was by now an old member of the group, having chosen it instead of going back to therapy at the time of Isabel's abandonment. He was part of it and as responsible as anybody else to take care of all its members.

***

The man in the jeans and dark blue sweater was rather intriguing, Ellie thought. In her observations, men fell into two categories when in groups: either talkative and domineering or quiet and withdrawn, barely there at all. She knew even before he spoke that the man across from her to her left did not belong in either category.

She was not one to appreciate the silent therapist stereotype, and even less, the old-fashioned, formal style of therapy, so Ellie had every reason to think of Mrs Grahams as a truly unfortunate choice for facilitating a group of this type. She had been drawn to the name of the group, 'On losing and not being lost: a professional contemplation group', and she had naturally thought that it must be a rather quirky and witty therapist who had set this up. Now, she could hardly think of two words that would fit a person less. Mrs Grahams had not uttered a word since the beginning of the group session twenty minutes ago. She had not bothered as much as to introduce her to a group of strangers as a newcomer. She would have to sit this one out for the ninety designated minutes and she would never be back.

Mrs Grahams had deep-set penetrating dark eyes contrasting with the airy light grey of her linen shawl. Her silver-grey hair was rolled neatly in an old-fashioned bun as she sat upright, still, somewhat over-present in her silence. Ellie had to admit that despite her growing dislike of her, she found Mrs Grahams's presence striking, even austere.

She could not help but sigh quietly with relief when an older woman on her right started speaking. Her voice was steady, yet somewhat quivering. It looked as if she was not a frequent speaker in the group. She said she had a confession to make. She had lost, she said, all her patients in the last year and she was there to remind herself that she was indeed a therapist with over twenty-five years of practising experience. Jake, as the man in the blue sweater said he was called, said quietly, 'I am really moved to hear that. Thanks for sharing. It's not often in our profession that one is willing to let down the status mask.'

Ellie took a deep breath. It was her one chance to talk, as she valued honesty and unpretentiousness as few other things in life. Yet, would she have spoken up herself to reveal her own humiliating losses? This was at the heart of every therapist's worst fear, she said, one never knew if it was going to happen, and it was always a wonder to her that her patients came back at all.

'Well, but I wonder if you are talking of a personal fear here?' Jake said at the end of her speech. 'I hope you don't mind me asking the question, but it sounds as if you are suffering from a fear of abandonment. Does this resonate with you?'

Ellie could only hope that the blushing heat she was feeling all over her face and neck was not visible from the outside. And this time round it was not shame at all, but pure hot, red rage. How dared he? Did she really think he was an appealing man just a minute ago? He had barged in forcefully, interpreting her motives, doubting her in front of a group of strangers. Outrageous!

'Fear of abandonment', Mrs Grahams said ever so quietly and with hardly any movement in her face at all. 'What does it bring up for each of you?'

It had been just over a minute, feeling like a century, since Jake's rude question when Mrs Grahams spoke for the first time today. Was she saving her from the spotlight or shoving it on her even more strongly?

'Well, I suppose I must answer this, as I have been the focus', Ellie said without trying to conceal the bitterness in her voice. 'I am rather intrigued by your question and focusing on me, Jake, and wonder where this is coming from. Perhaps, fear of abandonment rings true for you? Having said that, I truly felt for the situation described, losing one's patients, one's identity. As far as I am aware it was the loss I was relating to rather than the abandonment, if indeed there was any abandonment there at all other than what you read into it for your own reasons?'

***

The tears came before he knew they were there. To his surprise, there was no embarrassment, just letting go. He remembered how his mother turned her back to him the moment he walked back from school, trying to conceal her alcoholic breath or perhaps to secretly sip some more. He remembered his first intense love when he finished high school, Lydia. They went backpacking in the Greek islands that summer they finished school. They hardly had any cash on them, but they both had the looks. They worked their way round most of the Cyclades, waitressing in bars where their English and fair looks were sought after. They were often given a room above the bar, small and dingy, but with the fresh smell of sheets that had been dried under the sun. They slept on the petrol-smelling oily floors of large boats, snogging under the stars, full of excitement at being about to meet the next harbour. By that time, they had developed a golden glow on their skin and the hair on their arms and legs looked copper-coloured and velvety. Lydia, who discovered during that summer in Greece that her name had a tragic Greek heritage, was, like him, an aspiring post-hippy lefty who grew all her body hair just like he did. She and everything else looked beautiful under the endlessly blue Aegean sky until one night, when she was working a late shift, he went to look for her and caught her kissing the dark and muscly Greek owner of the beach bar while sharing a cigarette with him by the sea. Nothing tasted or felt the same after that. They continued island hopping for another month until late September when work became sparse and they witnessed their first thunderstorm that made the soil smell of overripe figs and settled-down dust. Even though Lydia reassured him that this was a silly spur-of-the-moment thing that meant absolutely nothing, the guy was macho and not her type at all, as he must have known, they parted quietly upon their return to London – or rather, he stopped answering her calls. It was time that he faced up to it: he had no luck with women. He always brought out the worst in them.

It was the newcomer's astonished gaze, focusing on him with a mixture of guilt and remorse as well as curiosity, that brought him round.

'I am so sorry, I didn't mean to upset you', she mumbled.

'I guess you are partly right', he said firmly. 'I suffer from abandonment, but not fear of it, as it has happened already.'

He sensed the group's attention focusing on him, everyone waiting for more, but nobody daring to ask. For a brief moment he enjoyed the suspense, and the newcomer's expression of horror. It was satisfying to him that people sometimes reaped the consequence of their actions. It occurred to him that his mother never did. He always strived to reassure her that he was OK, that he was doing well, that despite everything he was unscathed.

'Maybe I suffered from fear of abandonment so much that by trying to control things and avoid it, I almost brought it upon myself. My wife walked out on me a year ago. We didn't survive babyland as a couple. At least, by now we have come to satisfactory arrangements about sharing time with our four-year-old, so I am not scared of losing him as well.'

'I am so sorry', the newcomer mumbled again.

He looked at her and decided she was attractive after all. He had unwittingly blocked her face out of his vision since the attack. Why did attraction have to come in this package of hatred and bloodshed a lot of the time? Could it ever be otherwise?

He smiled at her. 'You were right to go for me. You picked up how I like to focus on others to conceal the hurt. Again, trying to control the loss, but ending up making things worse for me. I've been coming to the group for almost a year now. I enjoy it and get a lot out of it, yet I had never shared what brought me here. My wife leaving me. Isabel, my wife not loving me any more.'

***

Fifty shades of shame, this was what her experience of sitting among this group of strangers on an early spring Saturday morning felt like. First nobody bothered to acknowledge her, then being put on the spot for no reason, then causing the collapse of an established member of the group; the man with the gentle blue eyes which matched his jeans sitting on her left was now weeping like a baby. Just a minute ago, he had seemed to her so together that for a split second, without even realising that this was what she was thinking at all, she had allocated him the role of rescuing her from all the pain, all the loss, the role of the one who could make her complete again, like a child forgetting herself on a rocking swing. She steered her gaze from him, hoping that he could see how sorry she was, to Mrs Grahams, transferring all her hopes of being rescued to her now. She seemed old and wise after all, isn't that what everyone looked to find in a therapist?

Mrs Grahams had made no eye contact with her since the beginning, yet, as though reading her thoughts, she said in her quiet but crystal clear voice:

'Welcome to the group, Ellie. You are now already a member. I wonder, does fear of abandonment resonate with you in any way?'

While Jake was speaking, she had of course made the detour in her mind, the island that was her mother's favourite, which she had left her for, where she died on her, on all of them. Her fear of getting close to men, as they would invariably hurt her. They would either be distant and switched-off like her father had been or, even worse, warm, seductive and then letting her down for a crash. Luke had, despite appearances, turned out to be in that latter category, and the bruising after the crash had not quite left her bones yet.

'Well, I also came here after abandonment, I seem to be in the right group for that, but if I am honest, what attracted me to this group was the name you gave it, "on losing and not being lost", as it made me think that all we can do as therapists and also as human beings is to be there for each other in our losses.'

'What do you mean? Commiserating?' the older woman who had bravely admitted to losing all her patients intercepted.

Ellie paused. She seemed to have attracted enough hostility from her fellow group members already. She always had a talent for that, but if she was honest with herself, she could see it was the result of being combative. Better fight than flight had been her mantra since her mother's death, and she had fought every adolescent fight she could have with her father, which, as her therapist had said, was her desperate attempt to bring an absent parent back to life.

'What you said about your practice moved me, because it was facing up to loss simply and plainly, rather than trying to pretend it is not there like we all do most of the time. What came to mind was one of my patients who I am still seeing and I just have to bear living with uncertainty along with her. A year ago, when she first came to see me, she was diagnosed with an early form of breast cancer. She had a small, non-aggressive lump. She is in her fifties, a mother of teenage boys and a GP. Well, you would be surprised to know that she has chosen not to remove the lump and not to receive treatment.'

She didn't know if she imagined it, but it felt like a murmur spread around the room. She looked around her. Eight of them were sitting in a circle. The room was luminous, and right in the centre a ray of bright light had placed itself between them. Other than Jake, there was an older man in the group who seemed to struggle with laborious breathing, possibly the result of a heart condition or of his extended stomach that was clearly pressing against his diaphragm, or both. From his body posture, she could see that he was accustomed to practising yoga and meditation, which by definition made him uninteresting to her. Maybe it was yet another of her ways of going against the grain to be sceptical, to say the least, about the Eastern practices spreading their wings and blending with the newest psychotherapy trends. Did people need any more encouragement to turn away from each other, to glorify self-sufficiency? Other than these two men, the other six members were women, a good ratio nevertheless given the recent feminisation that talking about feelings had endured.

'Are you saying that your patient is suicidal?' a younger woman asked her in a sharp tone. She was a woman about Ellie's age wearing the ubiquitous skinny jeans that highlighted her well-trained legs. Her hair had been straightened that morning and fell like a smooth black curtain around her evenly structured face. Ellie had spent some time studying her features when she first sat down among the group. She always had mixed feelings about people who fitted in, admiration and contempt at the same time.

Ellie spoke. 'This was my first reaction too. I felt she was just doing herself in, I even wondered if it was legal for me to give her the space to express her feelings about her decision. It felt like I was colluding with her plan of self-destruction, if I didn't try to change her mind.'

'I see what you mean', Jake said. It felt like the storm in his eyes had cleared off, allowing some of the sun in again. 'We take it upon ourselves to accompany our patients on their journeys, even when these journeys turn out to be darker than we predicted and even when they challenge our preconceptions about the routes they should take.'

'Yes, exactly.' Ellie felt excited for the first time today. 'The only thing is that it sounds easier than it actually is, and this is precisely because, despite what we want to believe, we are not really trained to accept loss and to help our patients accept it as well.'

'But why should this woman accept an early death and losing her children, when she has something that by the sound of it is perfectly treatable?' the woman in the dark bob cut across her, probably not even realising that she was raising her voice. 'I am sorry, but my background is in nursing and I find this totally bonkers.'

'Carol, I understand you have strong feelings about this,' Mrs Grahams said quietly, 'but can you please let Ellie finish her thinking?'

Ellie tried to ignore the quickening of her heartbeat, prompting her to give know-it-all Carol exactly what she deserved.

'The thing is,' Ellie said, 'my mother died when I was sixteen of a mysterious kidney disease that she chose to disclose to none of us. She left my younger brother and me and my father for the last year of her life, going back to live on the island where she grew up as a child in the Aegean. She fooled herself that because we were both doing well in our public schools, being tied down by long, orderly schedules, it was OK to leave us to have the last year of her life as she wanted it to be. Or maybe she didn't care. I will never know. All I know is that the biggest achievement of the rest of my adolescence after her death was getting myself expelled from that public school, making sure I got my father exasperated, making sure I did things my way.'

She sensed the heavy silence around her.

'You must have been angry', Mrs Grahams said softly and for the first time in a long while, Ellie felt cushioned, almost cocooned.

'I was and in a way I still am. And I was furious with Karen, my patient, when she said she had cancer that was treatable but that she did not want to treat. But it was one of my biggest achievements as a therapist so far to manage not to hide my pain for my losses behind self-righteousness. Karen is taking a calculated risk for the record, Carol, one that she has very carefully thought through. She honestly thinks that she has a better chance of a good and long life without treating her cancer in the conventional medical way. My mother was different, but I think that in her own way she chose life too.'

***

He was floating. Rather than try to listen intently, to facilitate things, Jake had been lost in the beam of light that had placed itself on the pale grey carpet in the middle of their little circle. As he did, the newcomer's voice came to his ears like reading a poem. A little accent here and there, a few dark turnings, some strange intonation. Not everything needed to be understood. What mattered was that what she was saying, whatever he got from what she was saying sounded as strange and familiar as anything that had previously moved him and changed him had ever been. He thought of the story of Odysseus, whose adventures he loved to read as a little boy. His favourite bit was when Odysseus was coming back home after years of wandering round the oceans. How nobody recognised him other than his dog. To everybody else, he was a stranger, a beggar. It occurred to him now that his strangeness that was perceived by others was a projection of how Odysseus himself felt, that this was no longer home, and yet, it was in a more profound and truthful way than ever before. Listening to the ups and downs of Ellie's voice, the sharp interventions from members of the group whose feelings of strangeness and hostility had been roused, as well as the mild, soft interceptions by Mrs Grahams, was like an opera with the theme of an unfolding ancient Greek drama. And as for him, he felt exactly like Odysseus' dog: he thought he was the only one in the group to recognise a profound sense of homecoming in what Ellie had said.

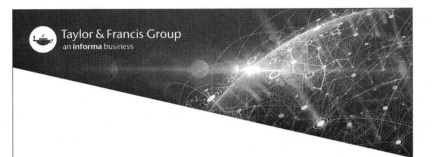